Alfred's Premier Piano Course

Dennis Alexander • Gayle Kowalchyk • E. L. Lancaster • Victoria McArthur • Martha Mier

Lesson 2B is available in two versions: Book with CD (#25722) or Book without CD (#25721). Level 2B continues the steady development of artistry and keyboard skills that began in 1A and continued through 2A.

- Note-reading skills are expanded to include additional ledger-line notes. Melodic and harmonic 7ths and octaves are used to help the student move freely around the keyboard.
- Dotted quarter and eighth-note rhythm patterns are added to other rhythms of gradually increasing complexity.
- Technical *Workouts* continue the development of skills, including one-octave scales, chord patterns, hand-over-hand arpeggios, and legato pedaling.

Lesson Book 2B is designed to correlate with Theory and Performance Books 2B of *Alfred's Premier Piano Course.* When used together, they offer a fully integrated and unparalleled comprehensive approach to piano instruction.

The Book with CD version includes a recording that provides a *performance* model and *practice* companion. Each title is performed twice on acoustic piano—a *performance* tempo and a slower *practice* tempo.

See page 49 for information on the CD. Flash Cards 2B (#25727) and a General MIDI Disk 2B (#23263) are available separately.

Edited by Morton Manus

Cover Design by Ted Engelbart
Interior Design by Tom Gerou
Illustrations by Jimmy Holder
Music Engraving by Linda Lusk

Contents

Theory Book: page 2

Premier Music Review

1. On the blank lines below, name all the notes.

a. 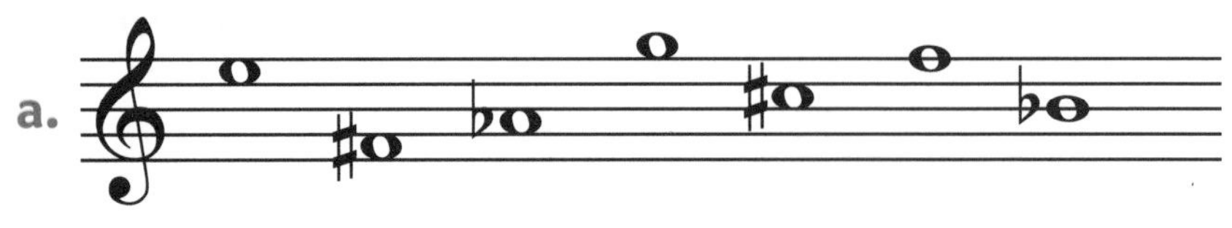

b. 

2. Write the counts (by measure) under the notes—then tap and count aloud.

a. 

b. 

c.

d. 

e. 

f. 

3. Name each chord by writing **I** or **V**^{7} on the blank lines.

C Pattern

a. 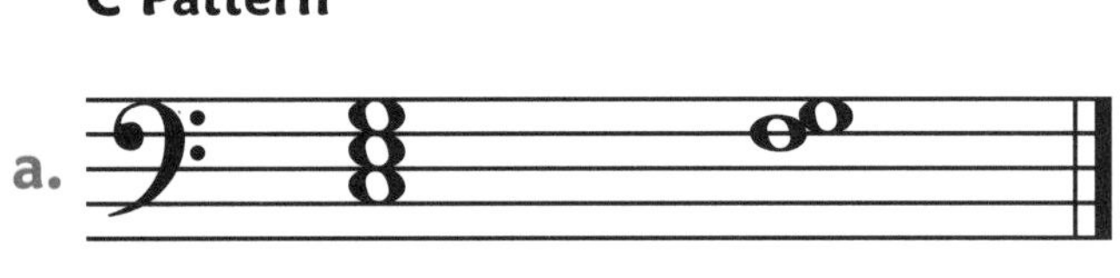

G Pattern

b. 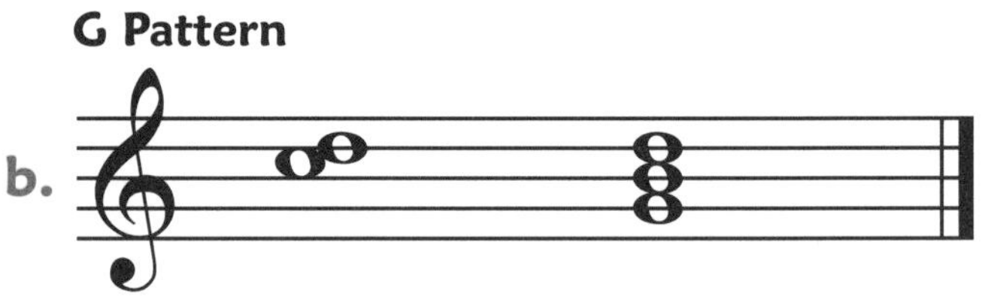

4. Complete the major 5-finger patterns by writing a whole note in each box.

a. 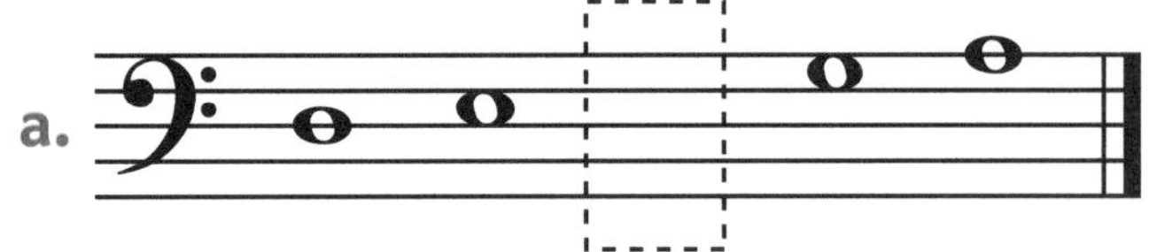

b. 

5. **Matching Game:** Draw a line from the term or symbol on the left to its matching name or definition on the right.

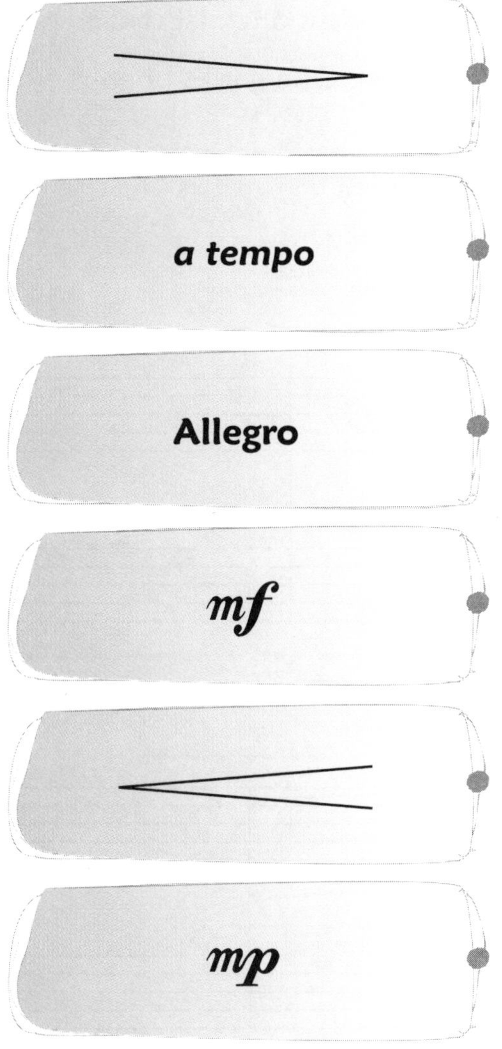

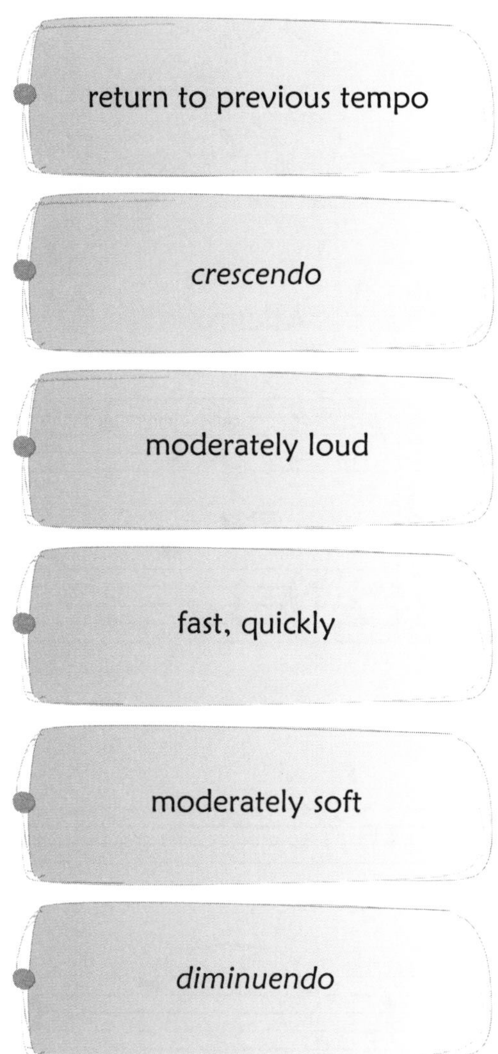

6. Solve the crossword puzzle.

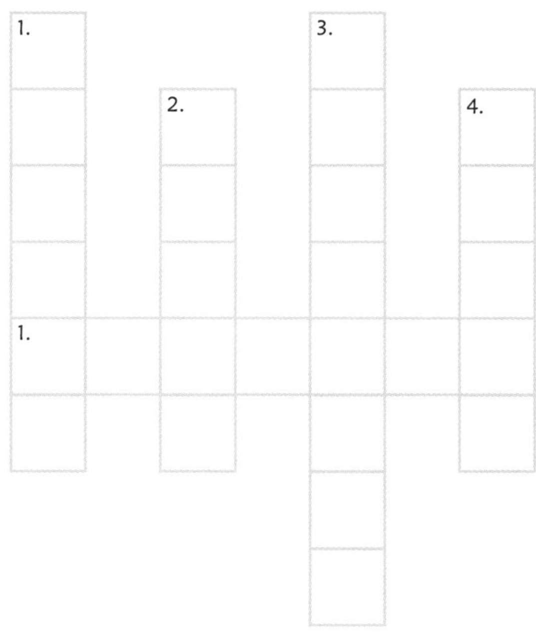

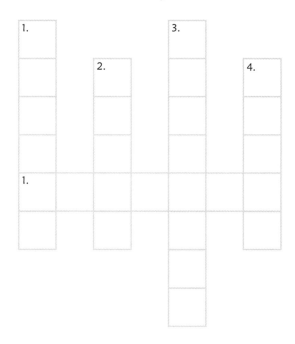

Choose from these words:
natural, sixth, whole, accent, moderato.

Across

1. The symbol that cancels a previous ♯ or ♭.

Down

1. Play the note louder than those before or after.
2. is the interval of a ________ .
3. Play at a moderate tempo.
4. Two half steps make a ________ step.

Theory Book: page 3
Performance Book: pages 2–3

Jazzy Toccatina

CD 1/2 GM 1

A-B Form

The first section of a piece of music is often labeled as **A**.

The second section (which sounds different) is often labeled as **B**.

Jazzy Toccatina is in **A-B** form.

Section A

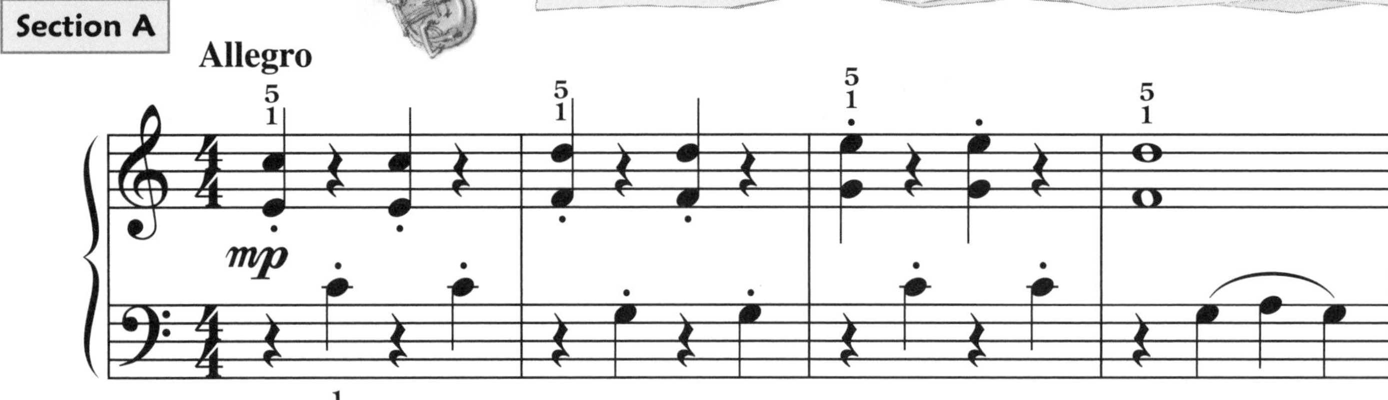

* A *toccatina* is a short piece intended to show off playing skills.

* In this book, selected fingerings are in red to alert the student to finger crossings or hand moves.

Premier Performer *Play the RH staccato harmonic 6ths using a relaxed, loose wrist.*

Theory Book: page 4

New Note E in Bass Clef

E is a 2nd up from D.
E is a 3rd up from Middle C.

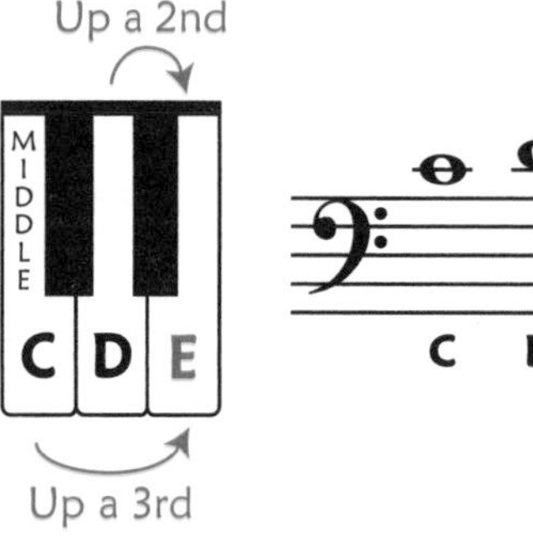

The Erie Canal

CD 3/4 GM 2

Go back to repeat sign and play again.

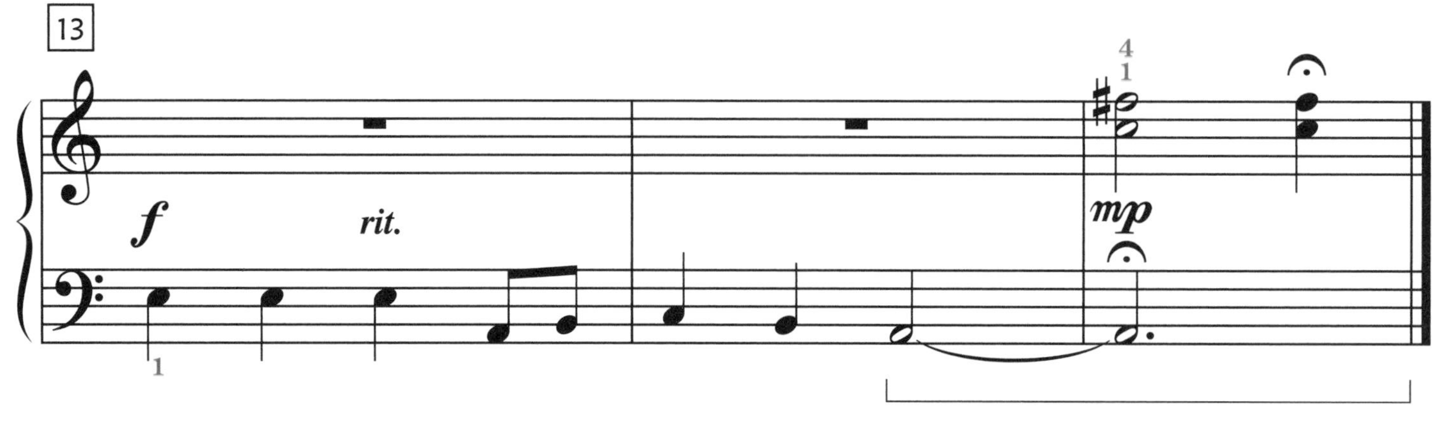

Theory Book: page 5
Performance Book: pages 4–5

Workout 1 Left Hand Moves

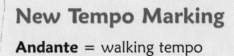

Play 3 times each day.

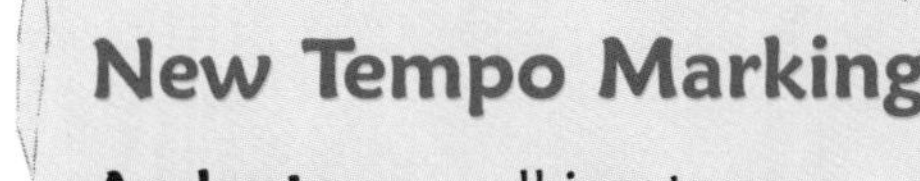

Enchanted Forest

CD 5/6 GM 3

Theory Book: page 6
Performance Book: pages 6–7

New Notes A and B
in Treble Clef

B is a 2nd down from Middle C.
A is a 3rd down from Middle C.

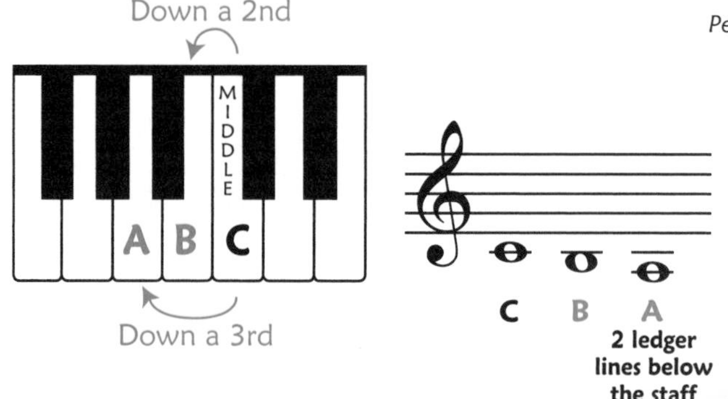

The Grand Old Duke of York

CD 7/8 GM 4

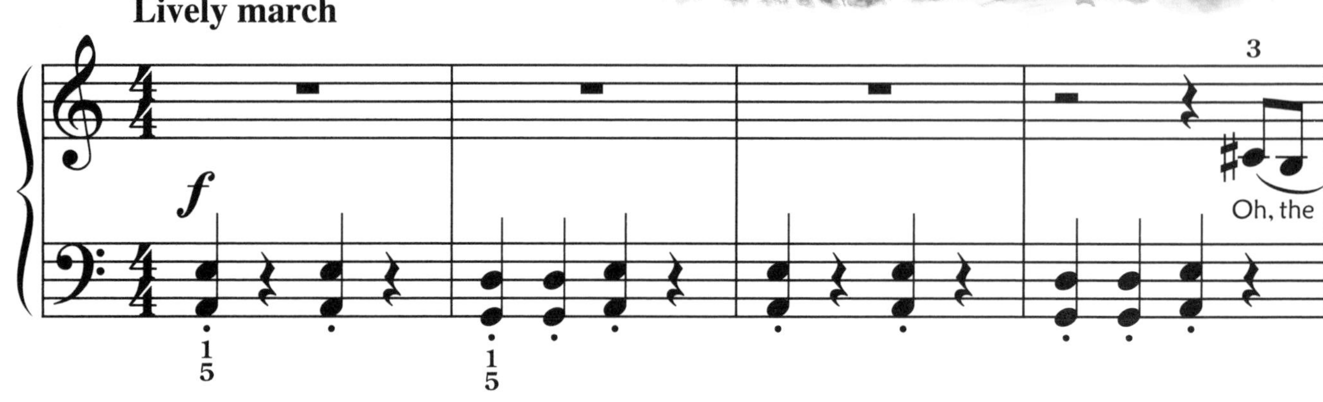

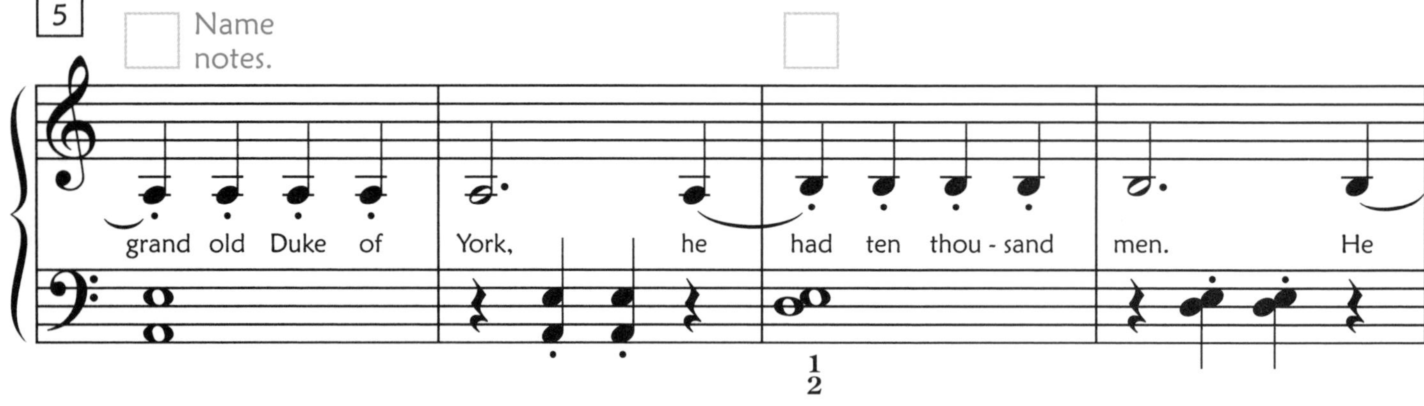

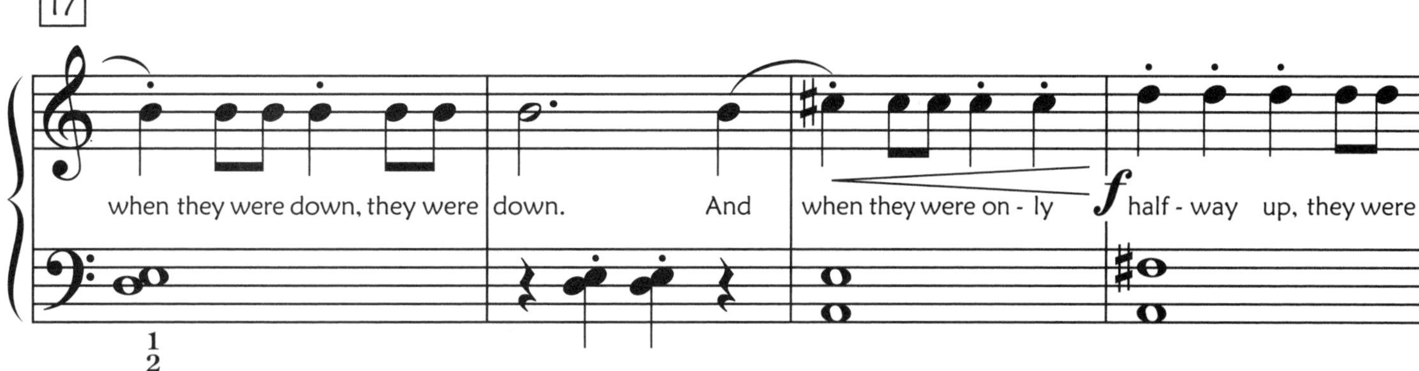

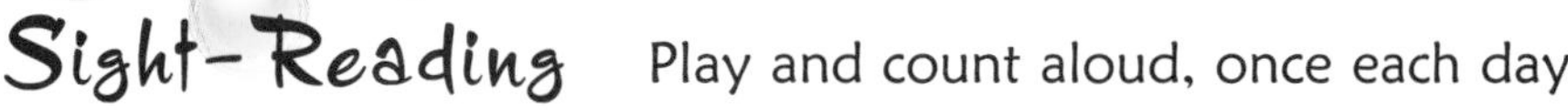

Keep your fingers close to the keys when playing the repeated notes.

Sight-Reading

Play and count aloud, once each day.

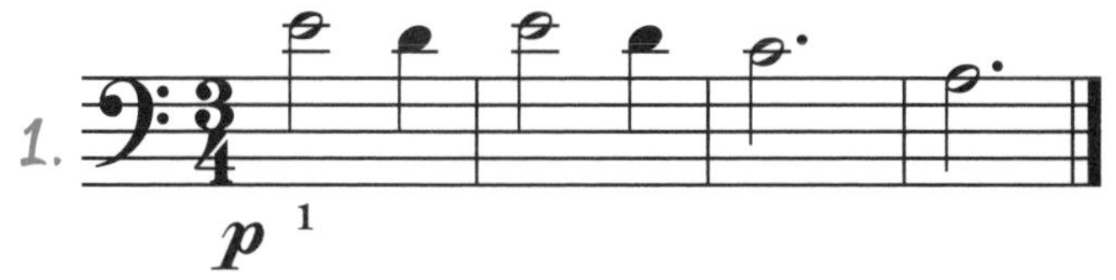

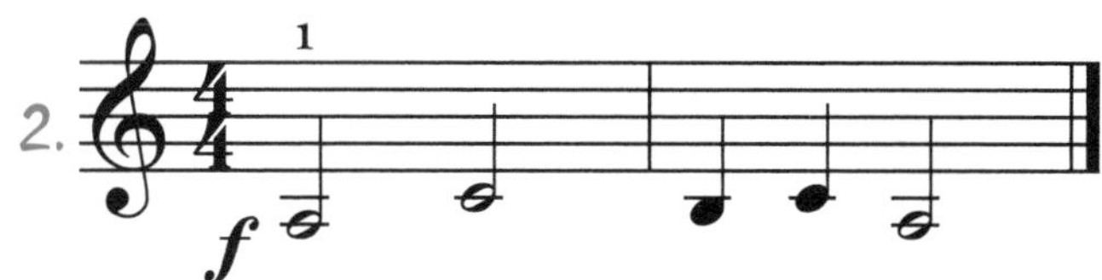

Theory Book: page 7
Performance Book: page 8

Minor 5-Finger Patterns
with All White Keys

The *minor* 5-finger pattern is formed when the tonic note is followed by a

whole step—half step—whole step—whole step

Play the following minor patterns hands separately, then together.

A Minor 5-Finger Pattern

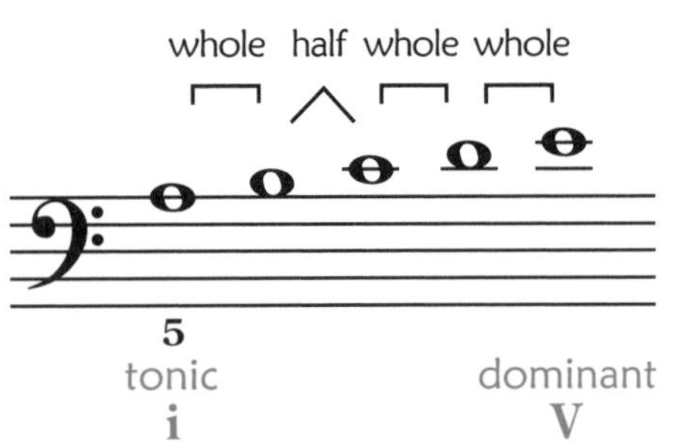

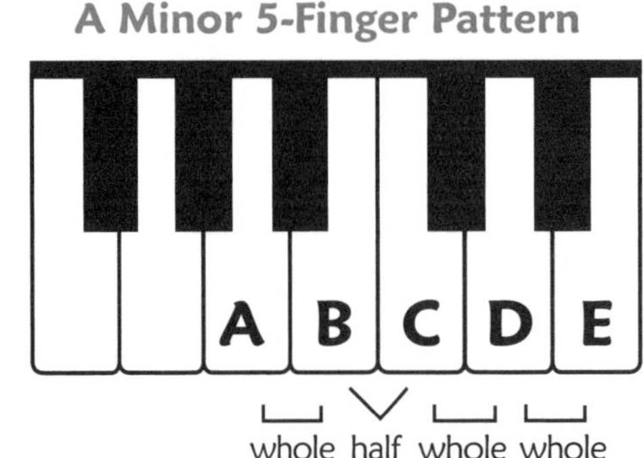

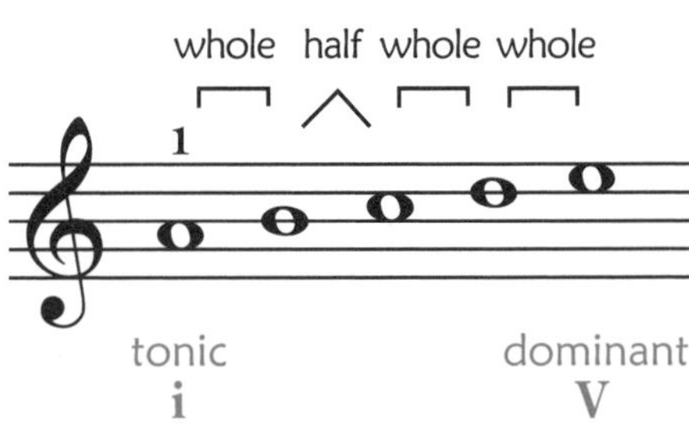

A lower case Roman numeral is used for tonic (**i**) in *minor* 5-finger patterns.

D Minor 5-Finger Pattern

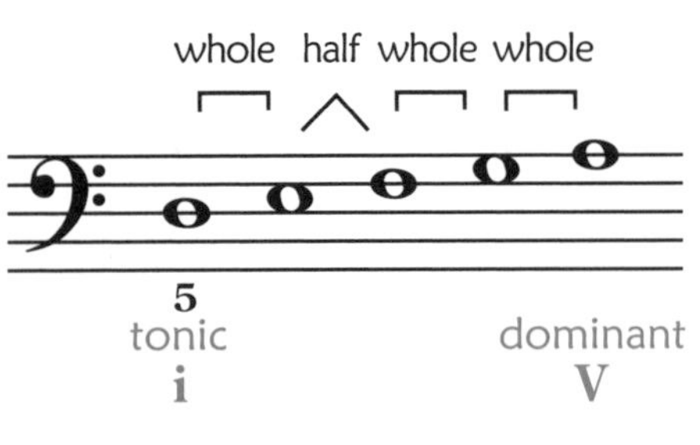

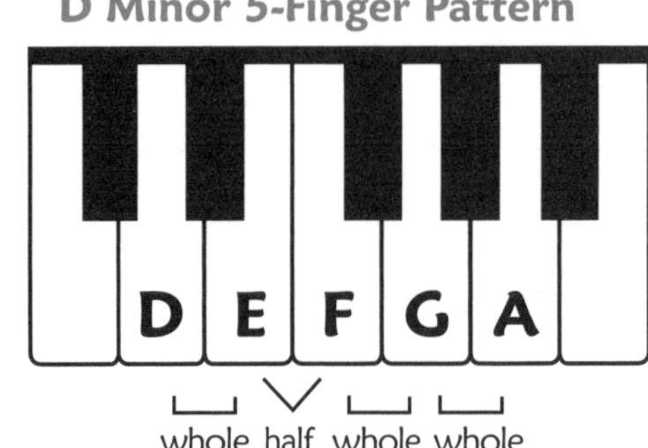

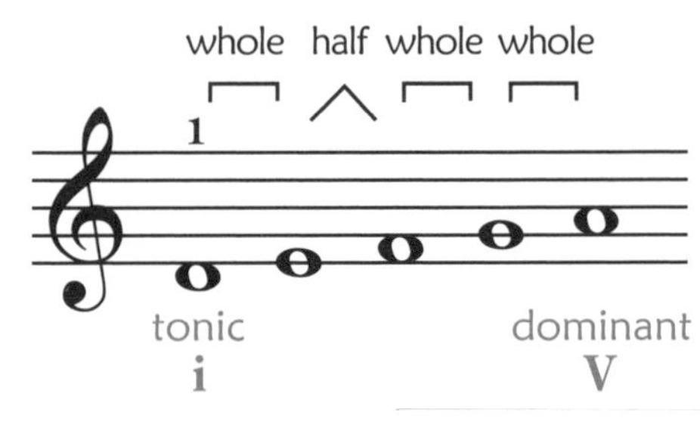

A Minor 5-Finger Pattern and Chords

Play hands together. Then transpose to the D minor 5-finger pattern.

Using this rhythm, make up a LH melody with notes from the D minor 5-finger pattern. Begin and end with D.

Theory Book: page 8
Performance Book: page 9

Minor 5-Finger Patterns
with 1 Black Key in the Middle

Play the following minor patterns hands separately, then together.

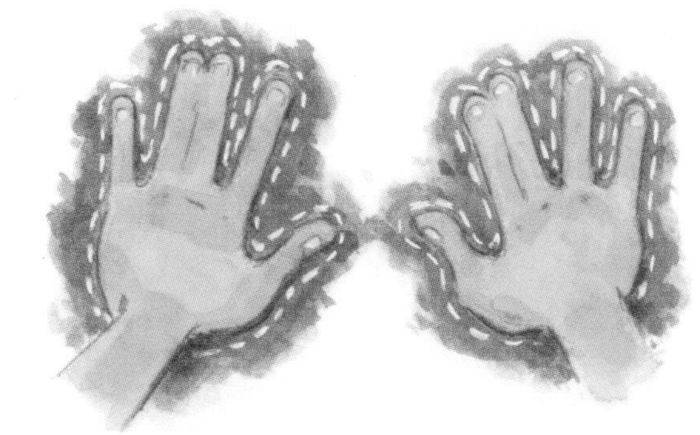

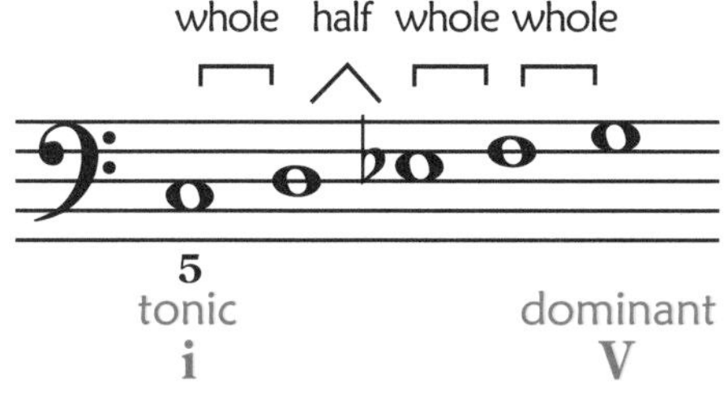

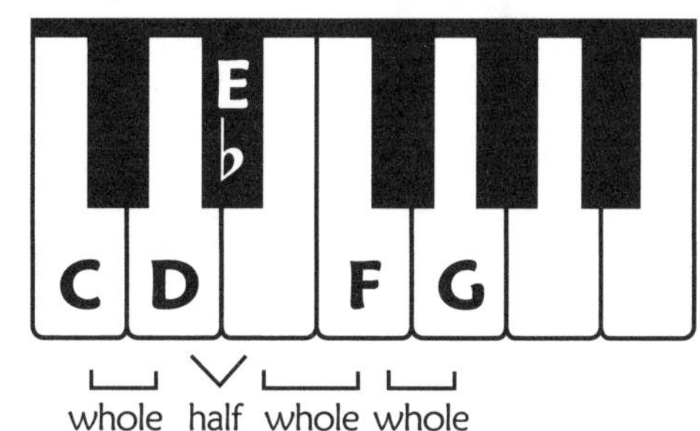

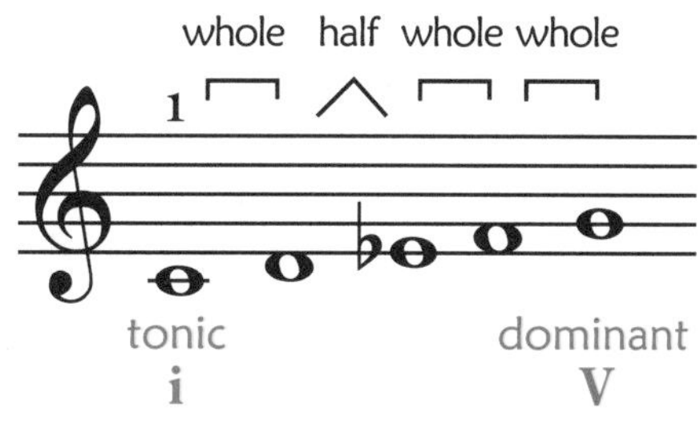

G Minor 5-Finger Pattern

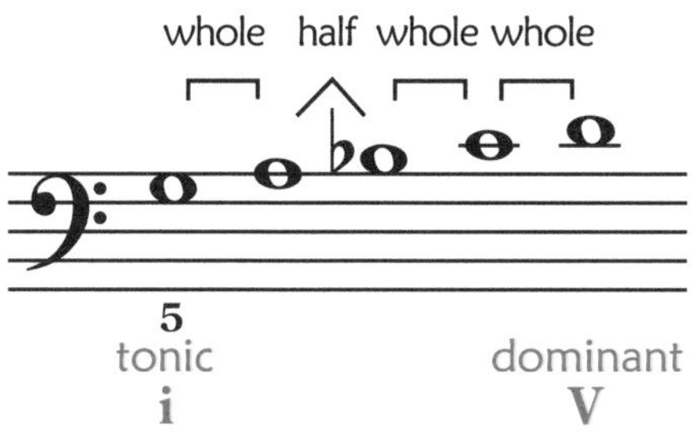

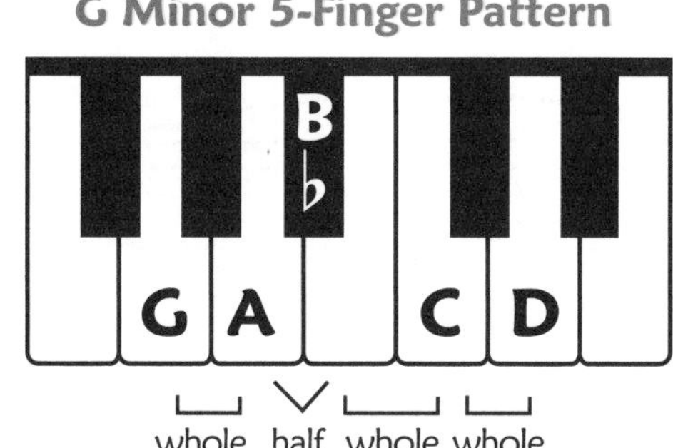

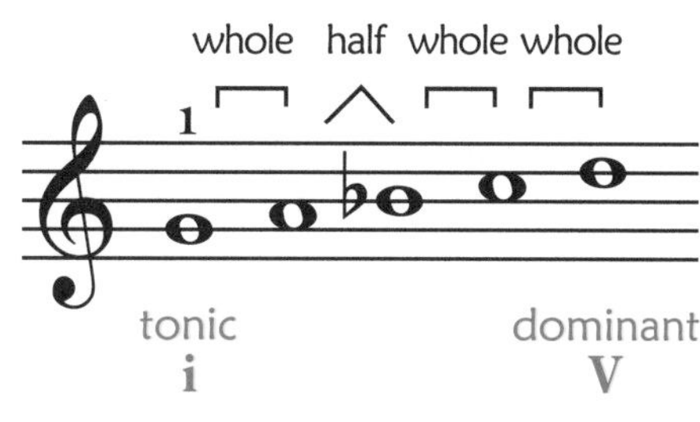

C Minor 5-Finger Pattern and Chords

Play hands together. Then transpose to the G minor 5-finger pattern.

Imagination Station

Using this rhythm, make up a RH melody with notes from the G minor 5-finger pattern. Begin and end with G.

Theory Book: page 9
Performance Book: pages 10–11

Workout 2 Major and Minor 5-Finger Patterns and Chords

To form a minor 5-finger pattern from a major 5-finger pattern, lower the 3rd note one half step.

C = C major chord
Cm = C minor chord

Play 3 times each day. Then transpose to G, D and A.

C major | C minor | C Cm C

1
mf
5

I i I

Rhythm Mania

CD 9/10 GM 5

Allegro

1 3

f

C

5

9

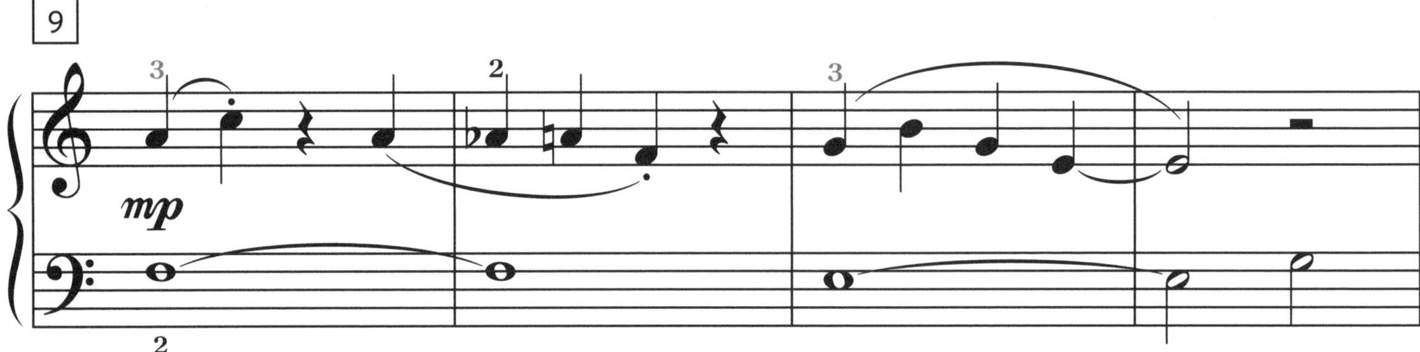

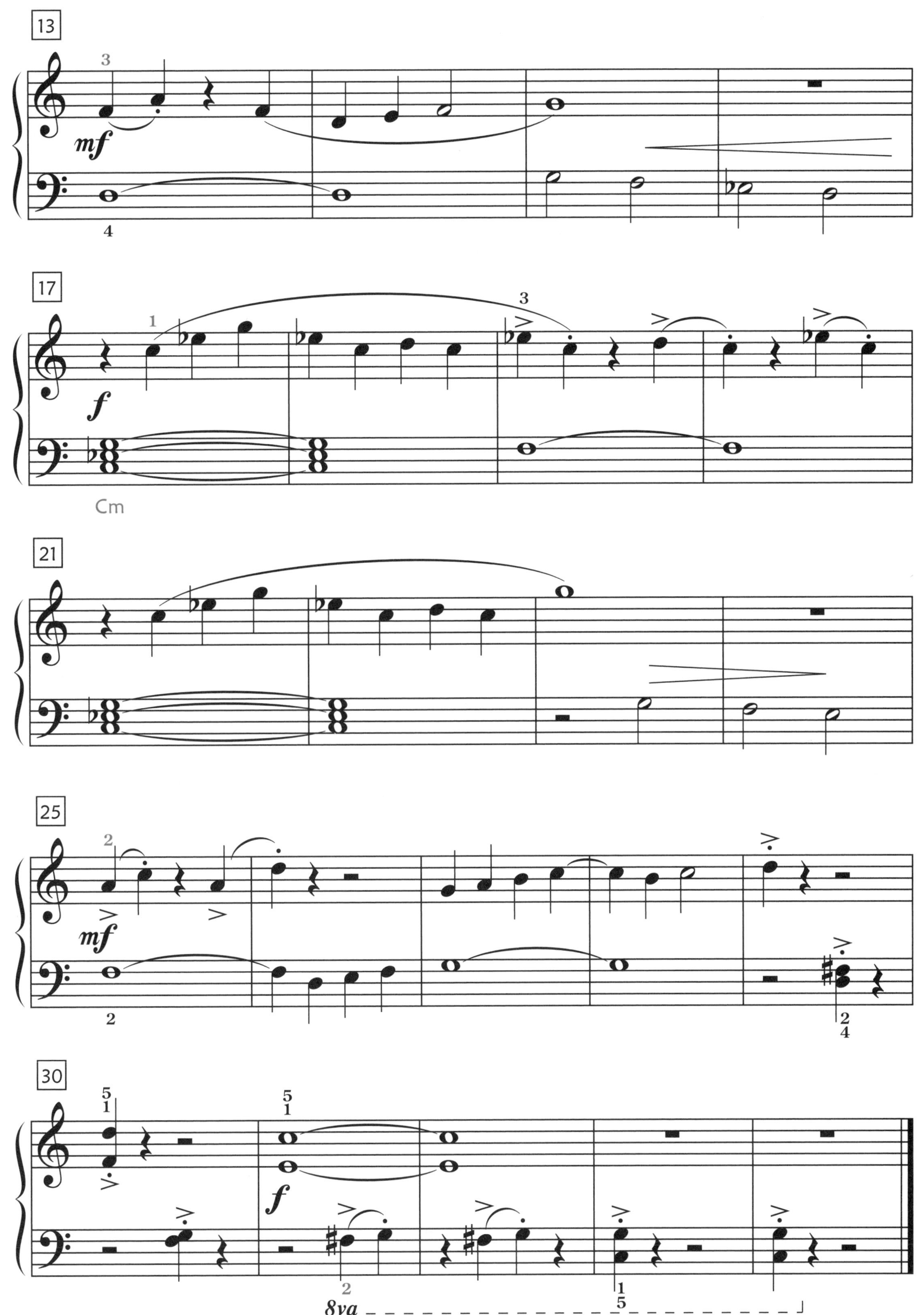
13
mf
17
f
Cm
21
25
mf
30
f
8va

Theory Book: page 10

Arpeggio

An arpeggio is a broken chord. Play each note of the chord one after the other.

Hand-over-Hand Arpeggios

(Broken Chords)

- Practice each arpeggio exercise 3 times each day.

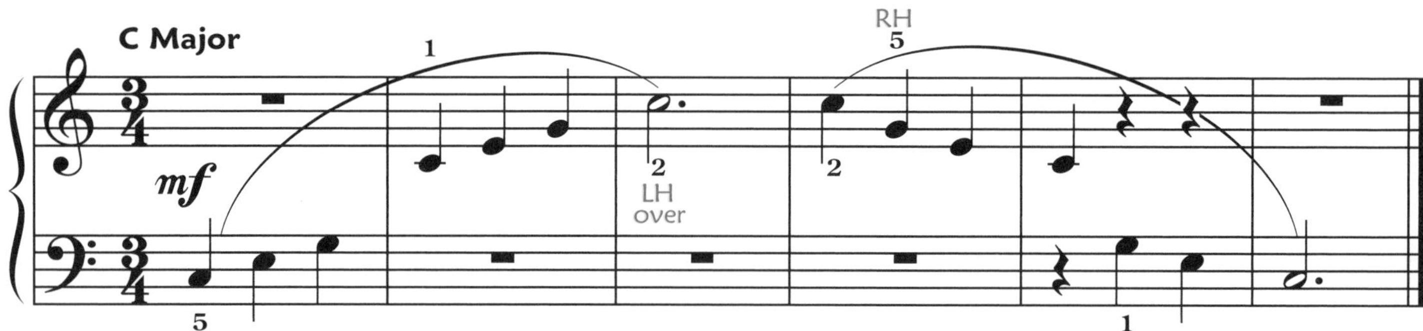

- Play again in C minor. In C minor, the middle note is ________ .

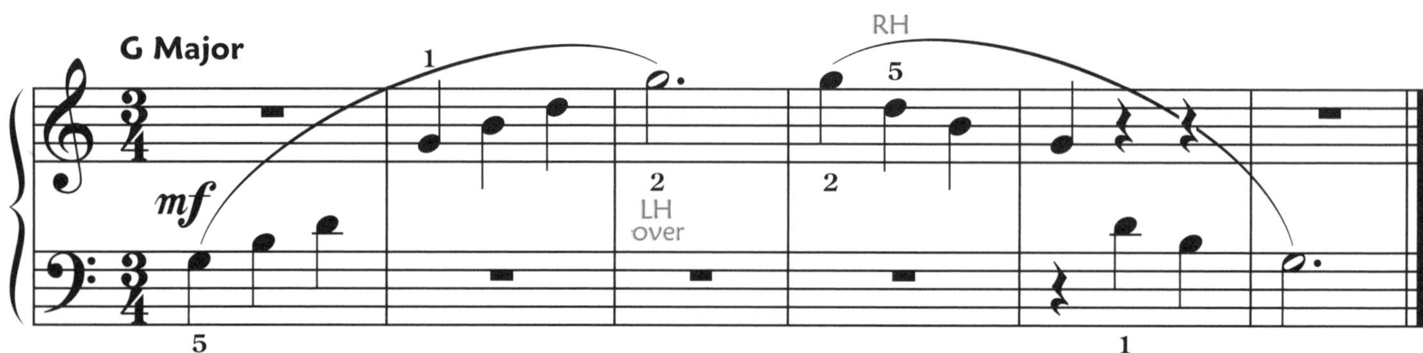

- Play again in G minor. In G minor, the middle note is ________ .

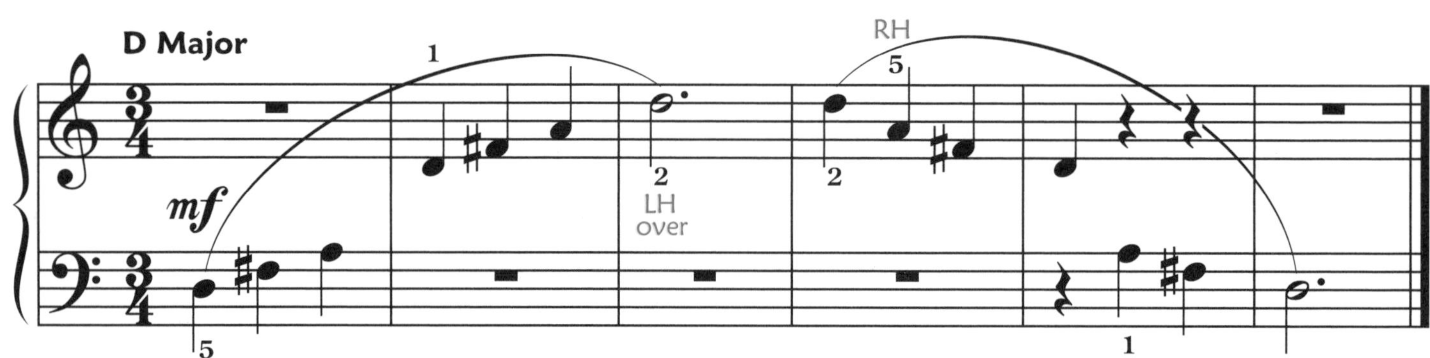

- Play again in D minor. In D minor, the middle note is ________ .

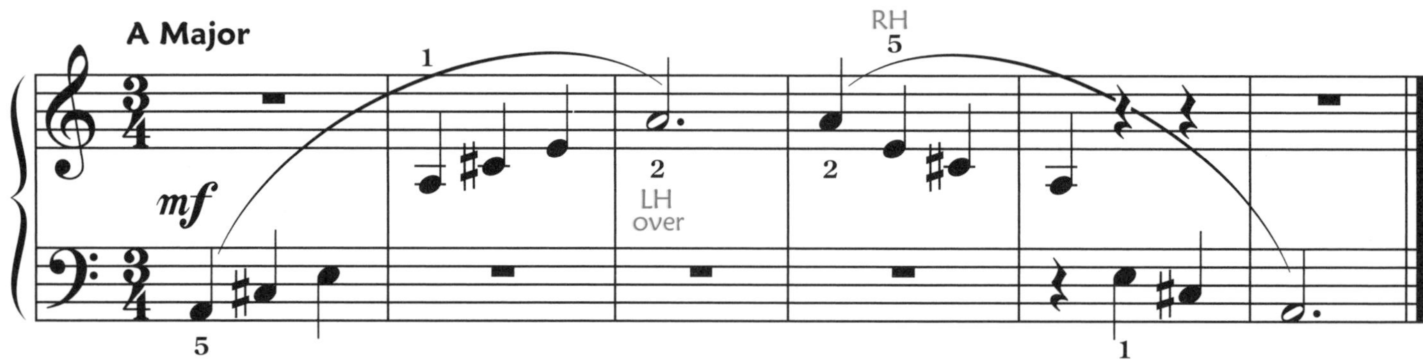

- Play again in A minor. In A minor, the middle note is ________ .

Medieval Faire

CD 11/12 GM 6

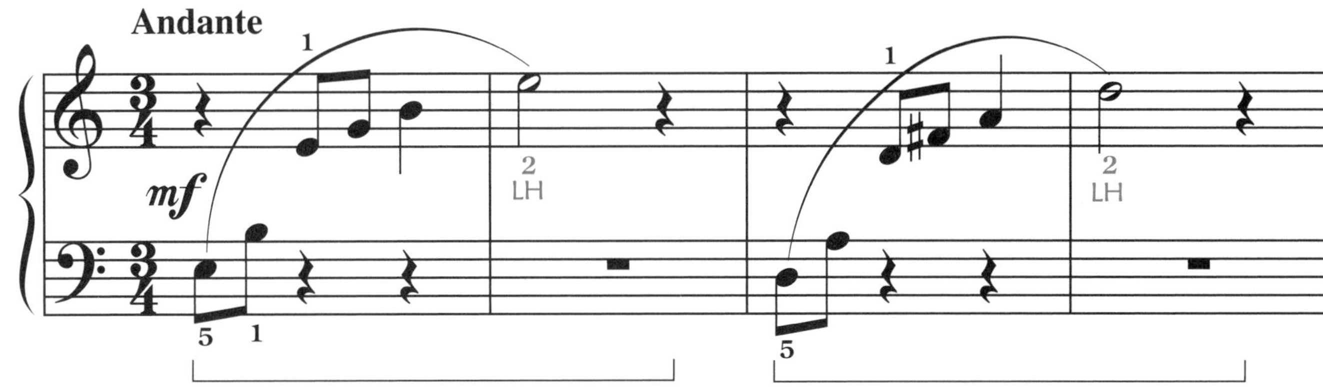

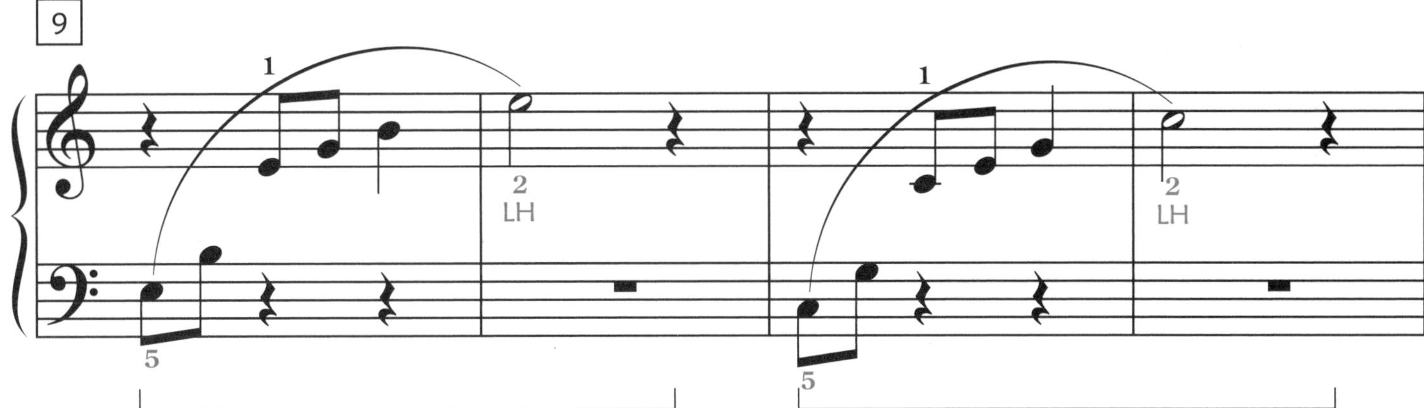

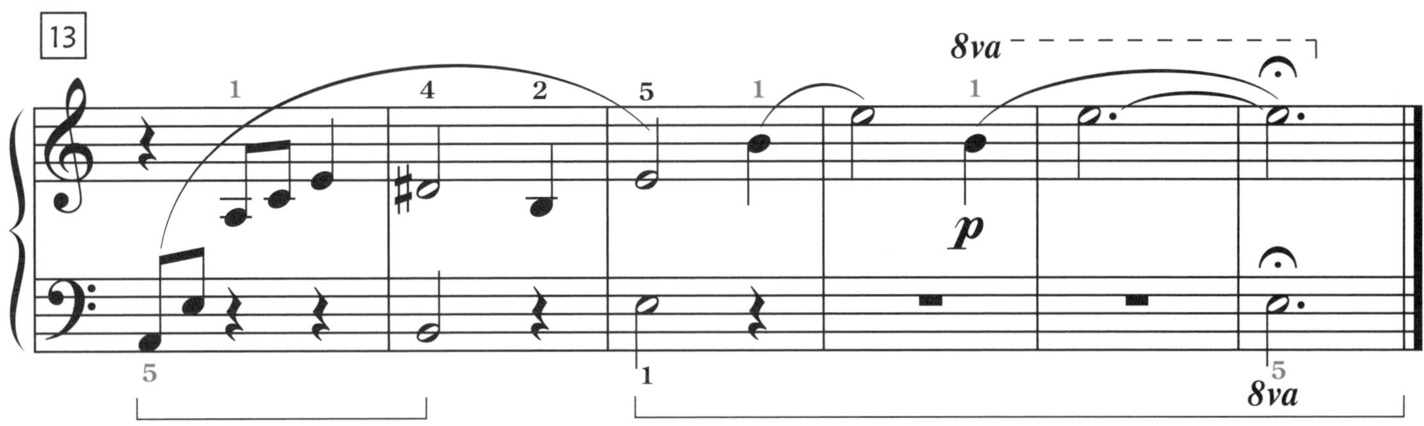

Theory Book: page 11
Performance Book: pages 12–13

f–p
Play *forte* first time.
Play *piano* on repeat.

Pirates at Sea

CD 13/14 GM 7

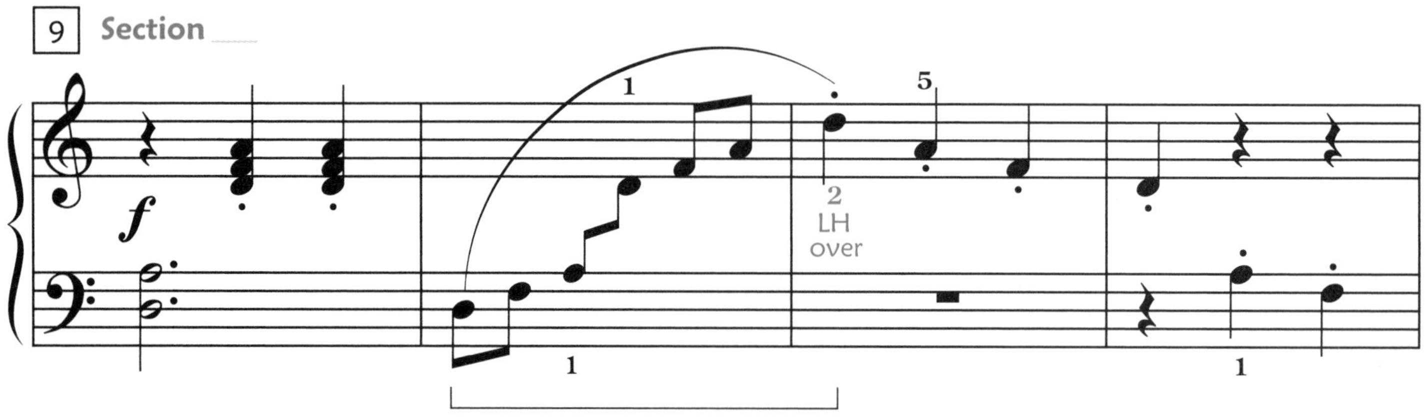

Closer Look *Label Section A and Section B of* Pirates at Sea.

Theory Book: page 12

Interval of a 7th

Written:

melodic harmonic

space to space

Played:

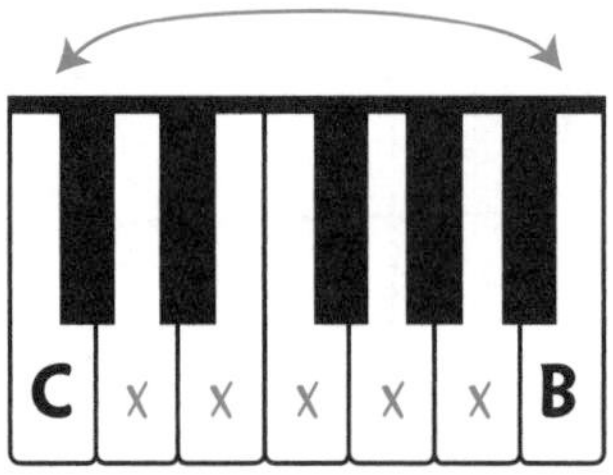

C x x x x x B

Skip 5
- White Keys
- Letters

Written:

melodic harmonic

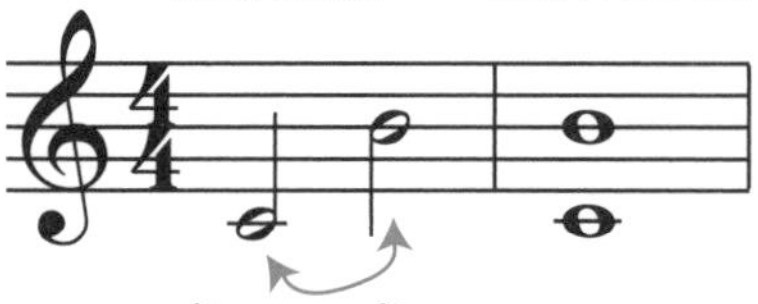

line to line

Listen as you play melodic and harmonic 7ths. Stretch the hand slightly to play a 7th.

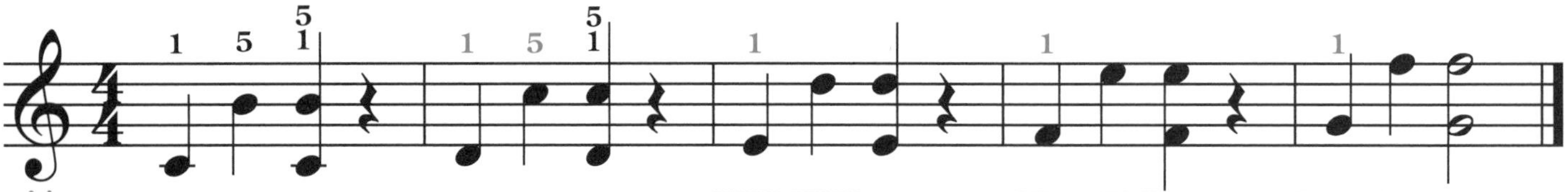

Name notes

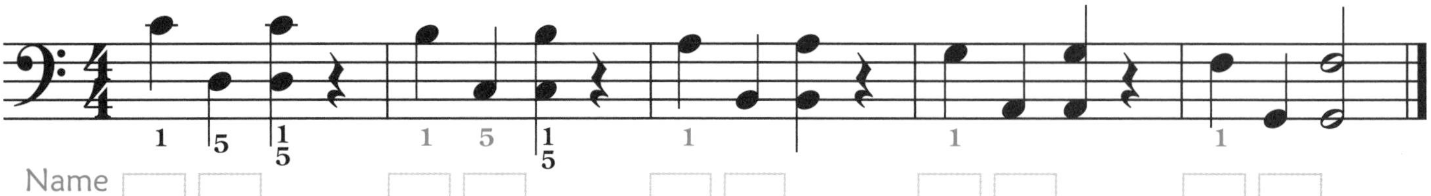

Name notes

7th Inning Stretch

CD 15/16 GM 8

Moderato

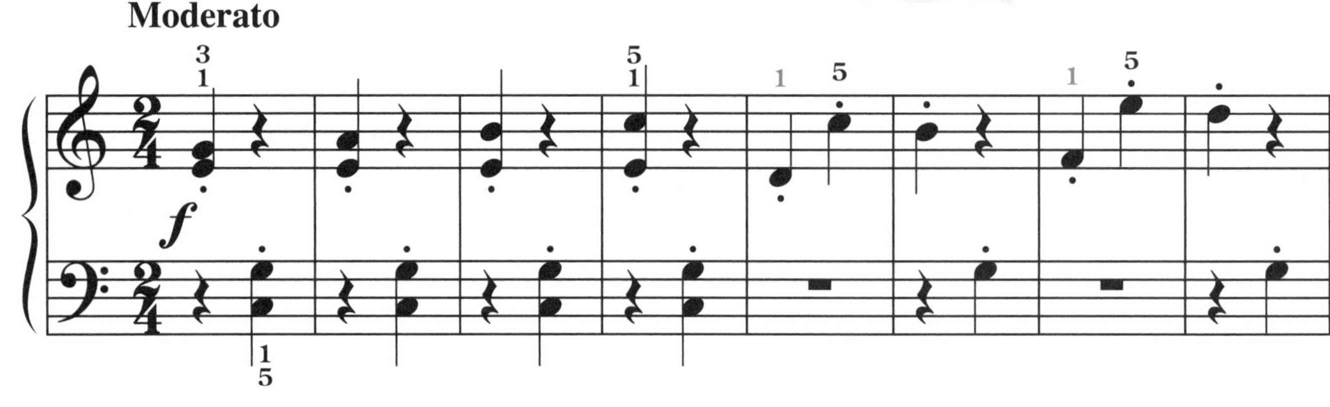

Theory Book: page 13
Performance Book: pages 14–15

Quiet Thoughts

CD 17/18 GM 9

Slow and thoughtful

mf

6

mp

11

16

p rit.

8va

Closer Look *Circle the melodic 7ths in* Quiet Thoughts.

Theory Book: page 14

D.C. al Fine

D.C. al Fine is an abbreviation for *Da Capo al Fine.*

D.C. al Fine means *repeat from the beginning (Da Capo) and play to the end (Fine).*

Rhythm Workouts

On your lap, tap each rhythm 3 times daily as you count aloud.

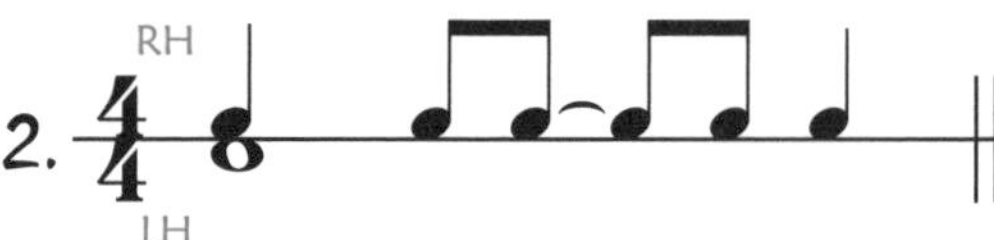

Premier Boogie

CD 19/20 GM 10

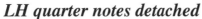

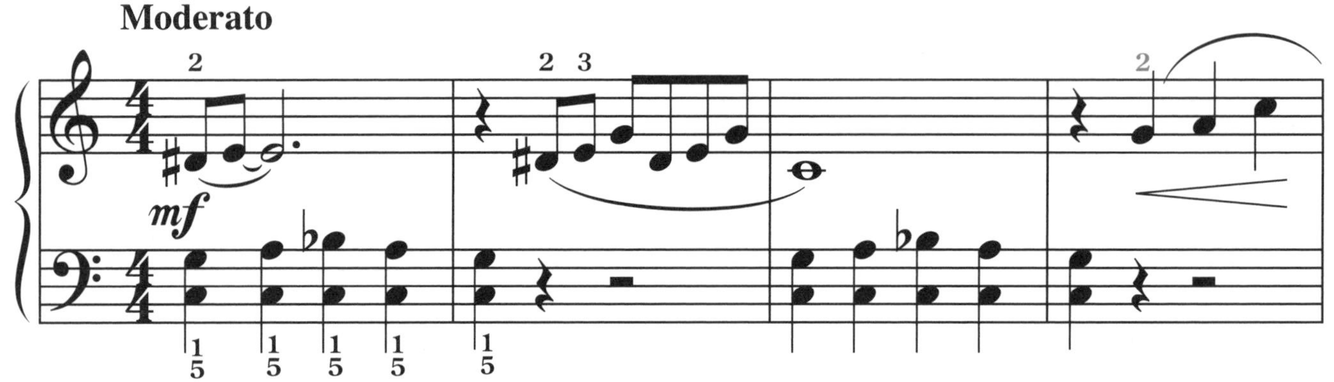

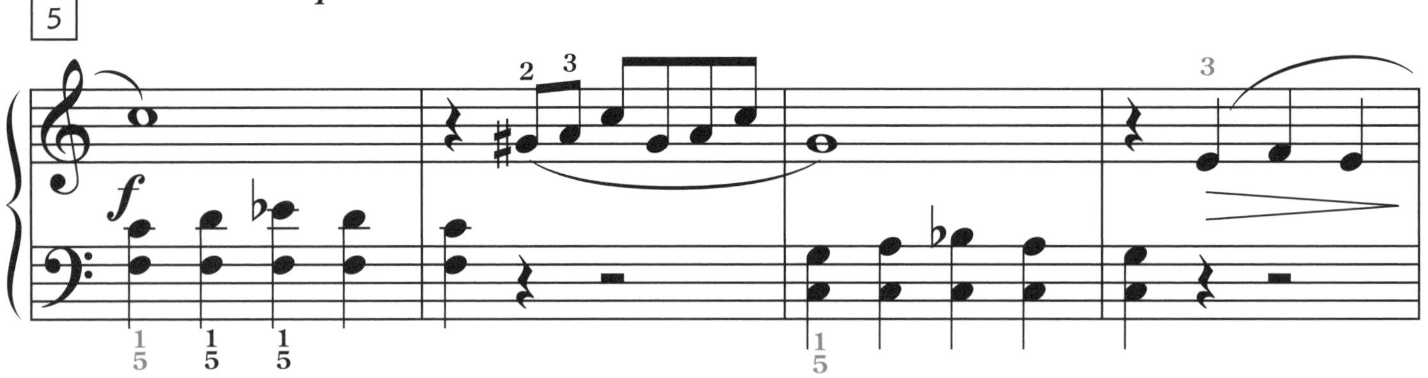

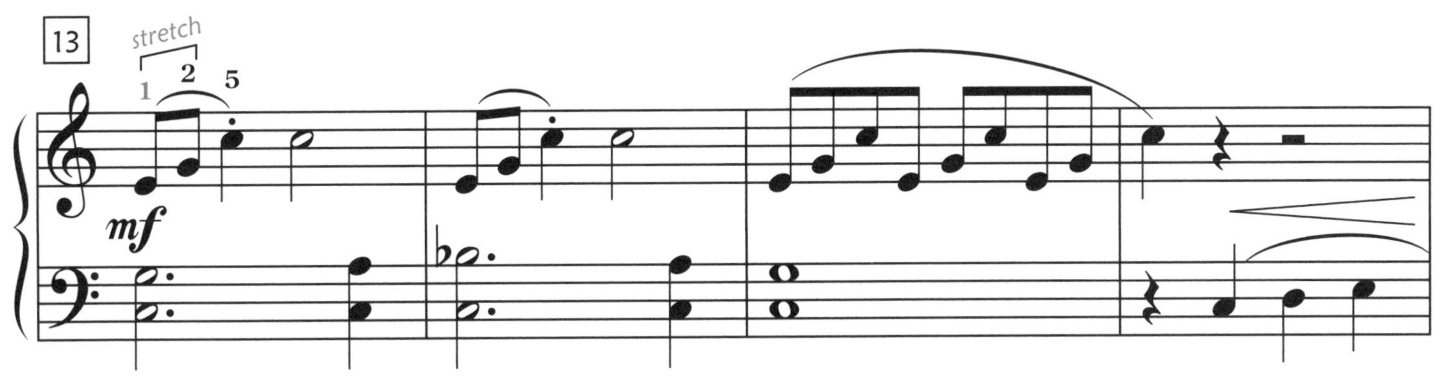

Closer Look

Name the intervals in the LH of measures 1–2 and 5–6.

Sight-Reading

Play and count aloud, once each day.

Theory Book: page 15

Legato Pedaling

When the damper pedal is pressed down, the felt dampers lift off the strings, allowing the sound to continue after the keys are released.

Follow the pedal signs to create smooth, legato sounds.

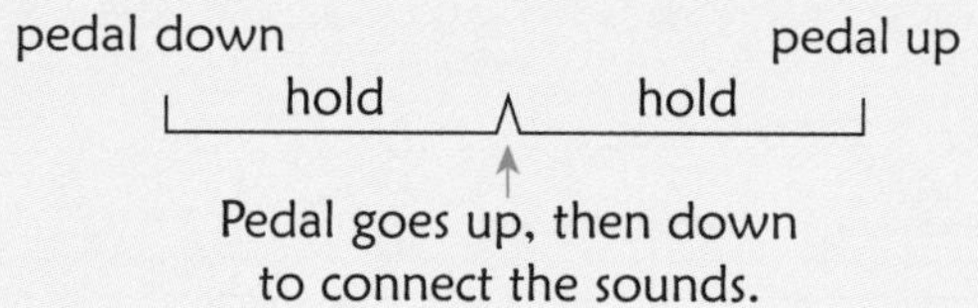

Reminder:

- Keep your heel on the floor.
- Let your ankle be relaxed as your foot gently pedals up and down.

Workout 3 **Legato Pedal**

1. Measure 1: Pedal *down* on 1st beat and hold.
2. Measures 2–5: Pedal *up* on 1st beat as you play the chord; pedal *down* on 2nd beat as you hold the chord.
3. Count *up-down* in quarter-note rhythm as you play.
4. Move your hand up or down to the next chord on the 3rd beat.

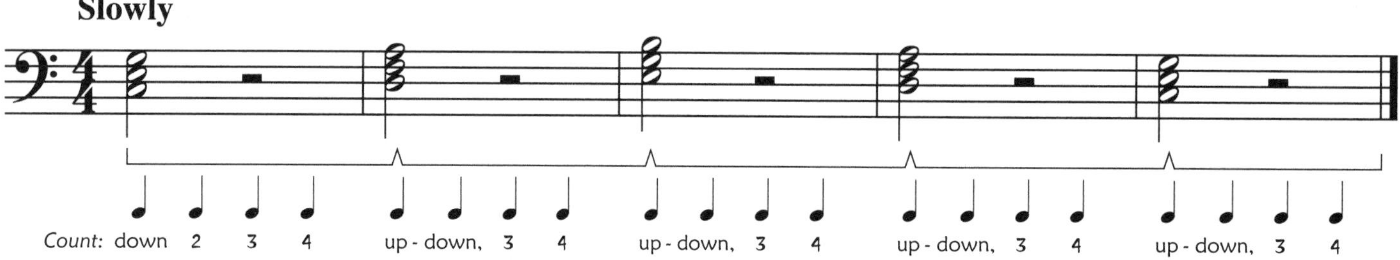

Workout 4 **More Legato Pedal**

Workout 4 is the same as Workout 3 but now pedal more quickly.
Count *up-down* in eighth-note rhythm as you play.

Theory Book: page 16
Performance Book: pages 16–17

New Dynamic Sign

pp (pianissimo)
means *very soft*

Lotus Blossoms

CD 21/22 GM 11

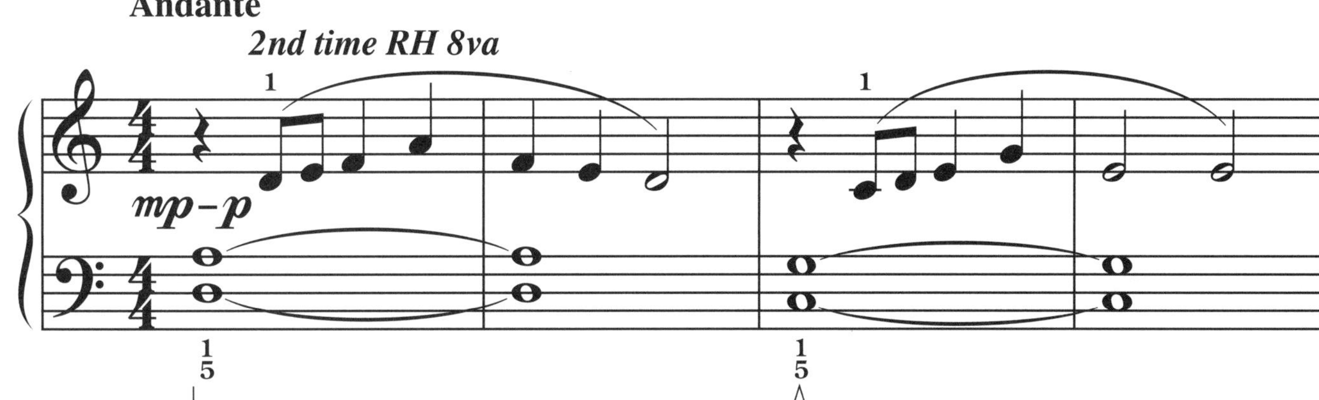

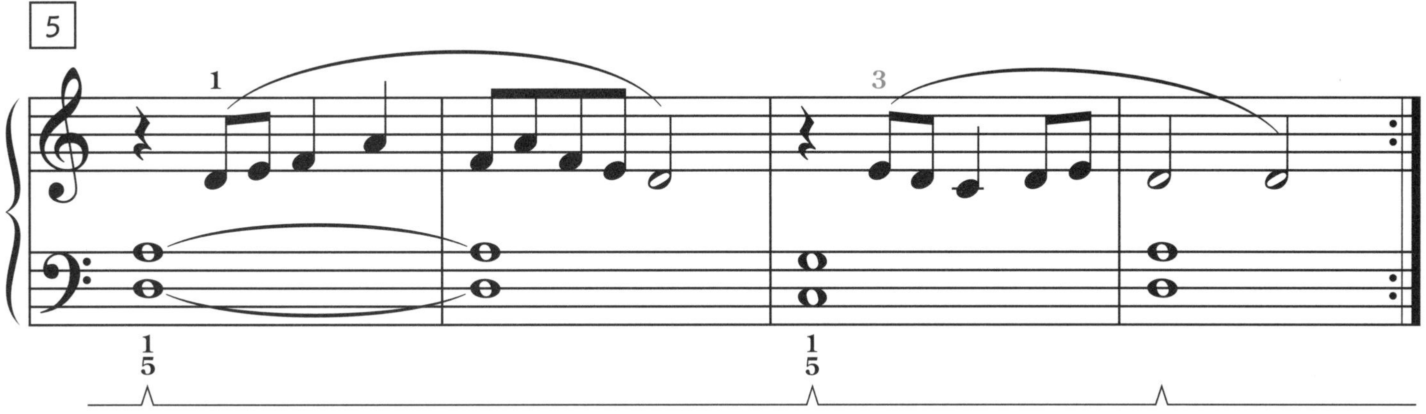

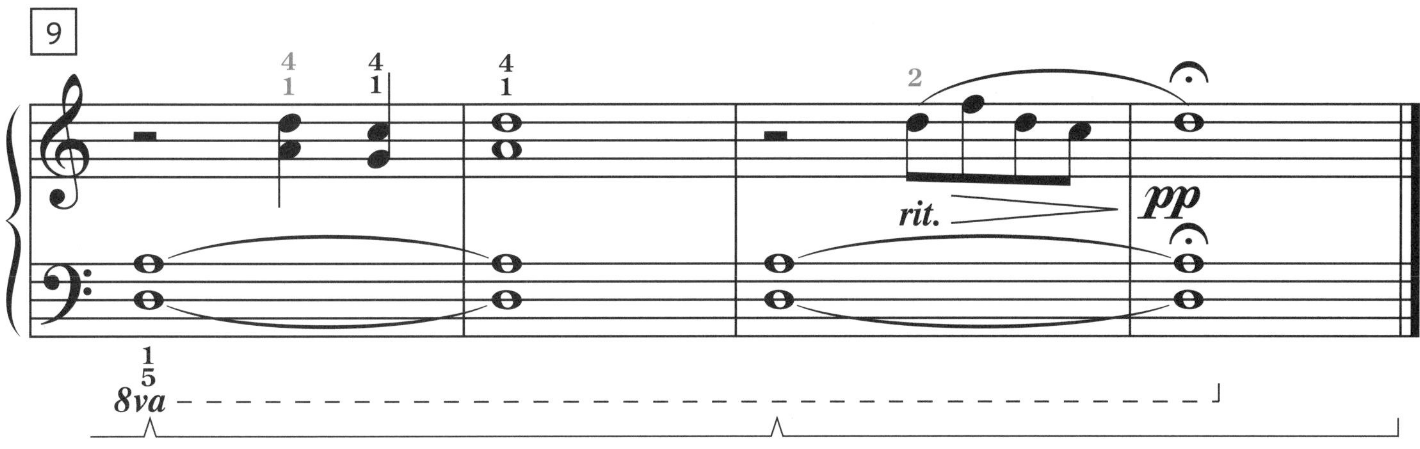

Premier Performer *Listen carefully for legato pedal changes.*

Interval of an Octave (8th)

Theory Book: page 17

An octave is the distance from one note to the next note with the same letter name (up or down).

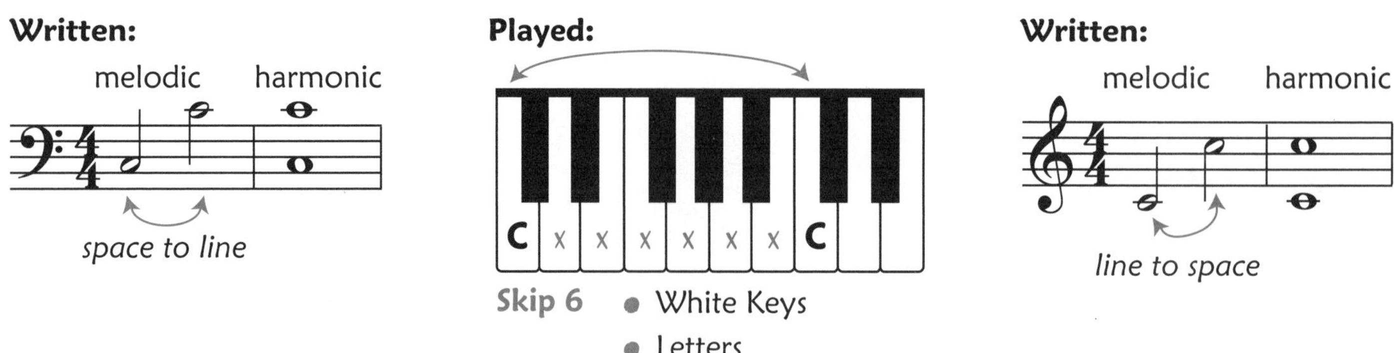

Listen as you play melodic and harmonic octaves. Stretch the hand slightly to play an octave. Students with small hands should not play the top note of the harmonic octave.

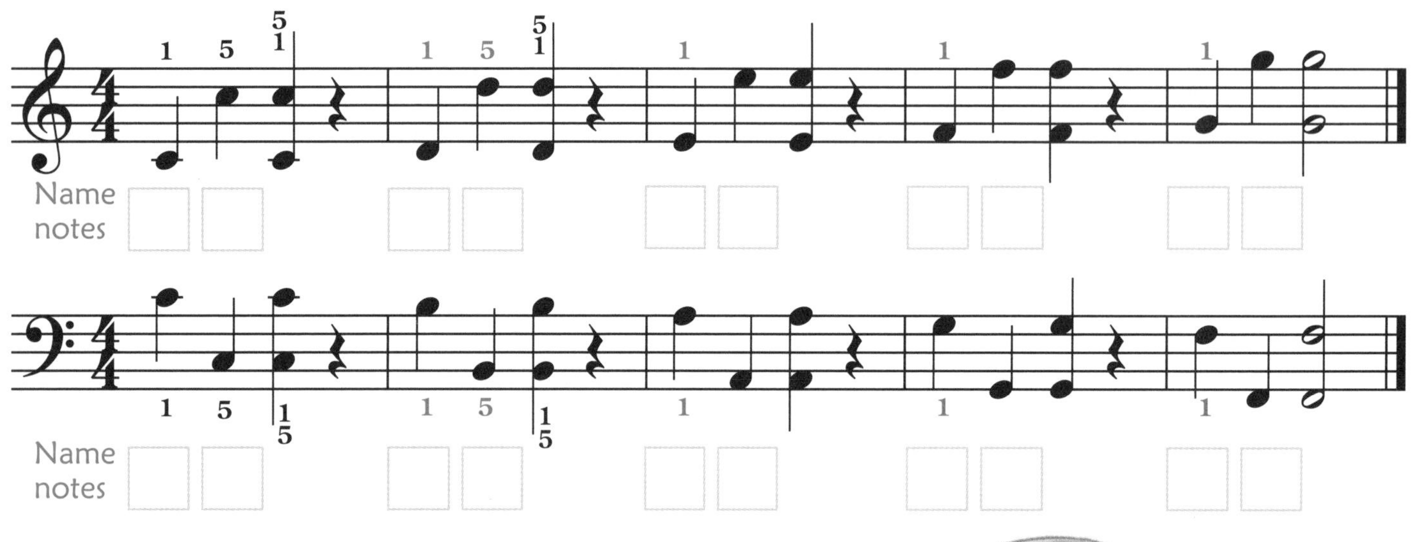

Moving in Octaves to Find Five C's

Each of the five C's are an octave apart.
Play them with RH finger 3. Then play again with LH finger 2.

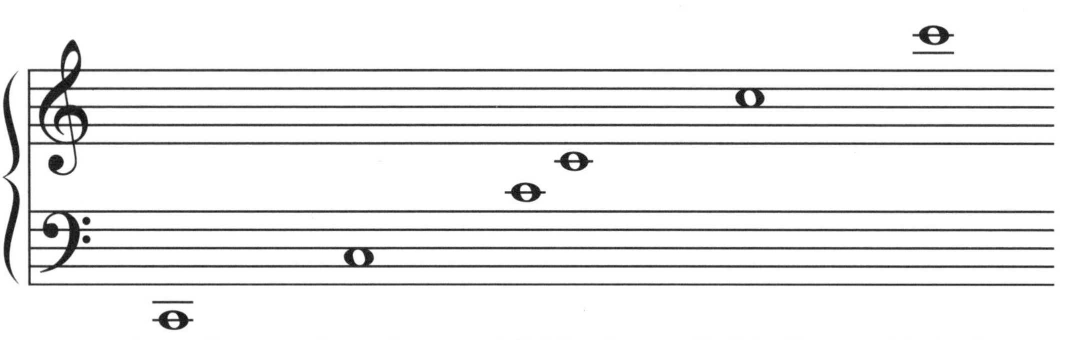

High C is 2 ledger lines *above* the treble staff.

Low C is 2 ledger lines *below* the bass staff.

Performance Book: pages 18–19

Science Fair

CD 23/24 GM 12

New Dynamic Sign

ff (fortissimo) means very loud

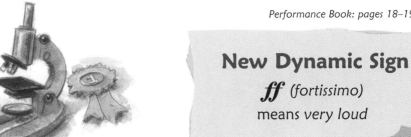

Moderato
3 2 3 5
mf
Pos-ters ev-'ry-where
at the Sci-ence Fair,
top - ics, pro-jects,
things to com-pare;
1
5
2

5
3 2
p
judg-es look a-round,
writ-ing com-ments down,
here at the Sci - ence
Fair.

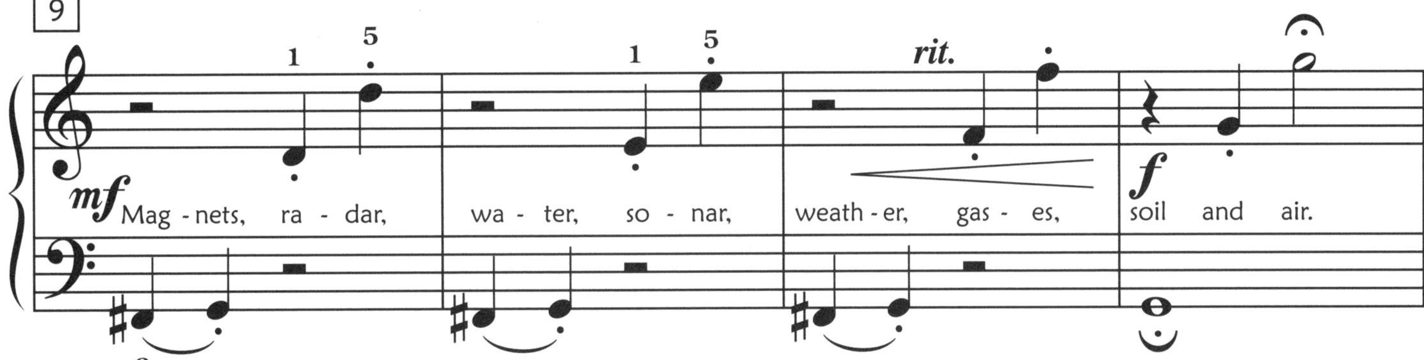
9
1 5 1 5
rit.
mf
Mag - nets, ra - dar,
wa - ter, so - nar,
weath - er, gas - es,
f
soil and air.
2

13
a tempo
3 2 3 5
ff
When the judg-ing's done,
we will see who won.
Look for rib - bons—
what do you see?

17
f
Red and yel-low there,
then we stop and stare—
blue rib-bon is for
me!

Theory Book: page 18

A-B-A Form

Floating Down the River is in **A-B-A** form, which has 3 sections:

- The first section is labeled **A**.
- The second section (which sounds different) is labeled **B**.
- The third section is like the first section and is also labeled **A**.

Floating Down the River

CD 25/26 GM 13

Gently

Section A

pp

5

9 Section B

mf

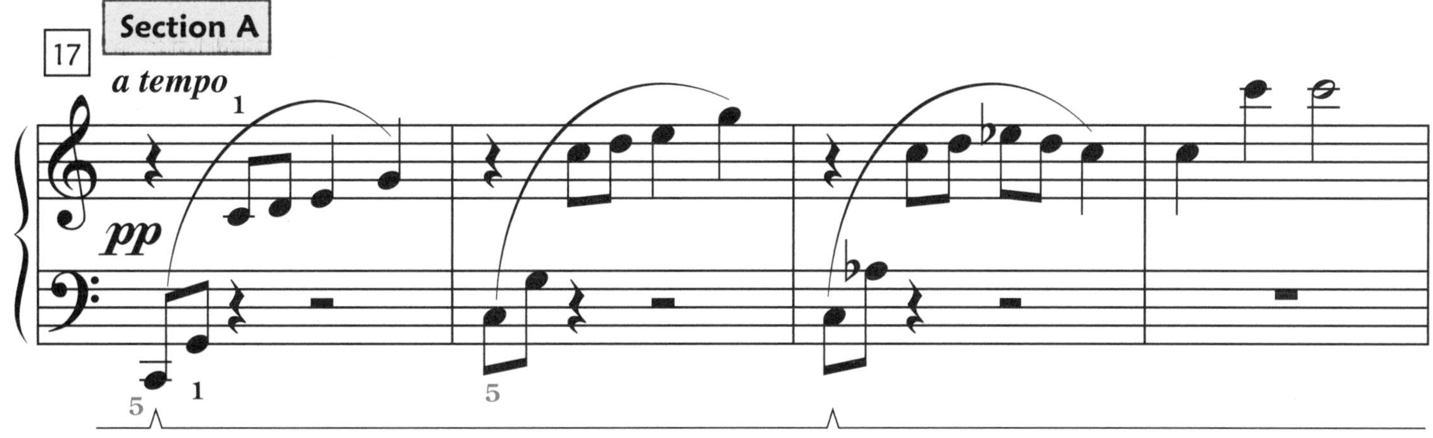

Sight-Reading

Play and count aloud, once each day.

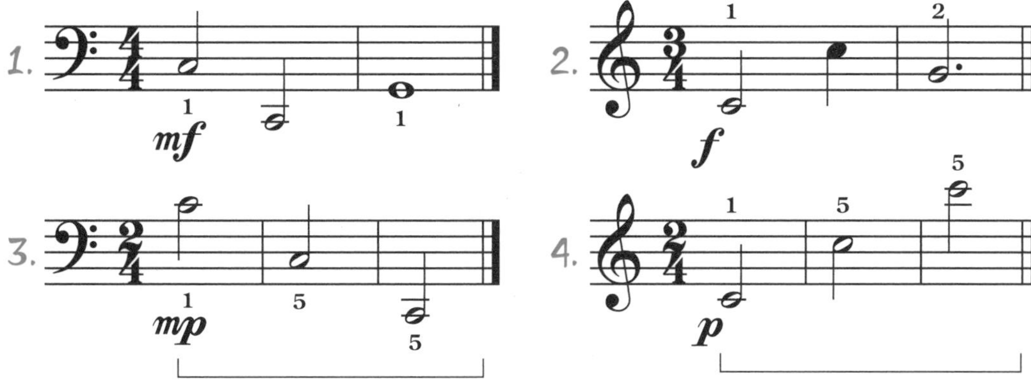

Theory Book: page 19
Performance Book: pages 20–21

***Richard Strauss** (1864–1949) was a famous German composer of opera, songs and instrumental works. He was also known as one of the finest conductors of his time.* Also sprach Zarathustra *was written for symphony orchestra in 1896. Its themes have been used in movies and cartoons.*

Also sprach Zarathustra

CD 27/28 GM 14

Richard Strauss

Slow and bold

mp *f*

6

ff Lowest G on piano

mf

10

f

Imagination Station

Using the 5 C's, create your own piece.
Press and hold the damper pedal throughout.

Theory Book: page 20

Workout 5 Preparation for C Major Scale

Play 3 times each day.

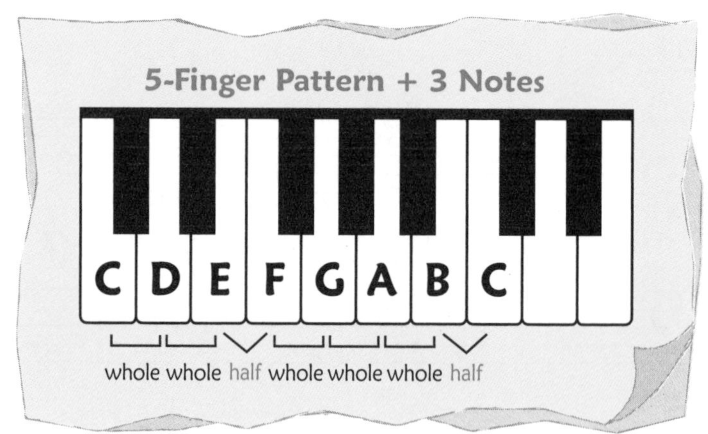

C Major Scale

The C major scale contains 8 notes—
the C 5-finger pattern + 3 notes.

Half steps occur between notes 3–4 and 7–8.

In the C major scale, there is no sharp or flat.

Playing the C Major Scale—Hands Separately

Say the finger numbers as you practice slowly. Memorize the fingering.

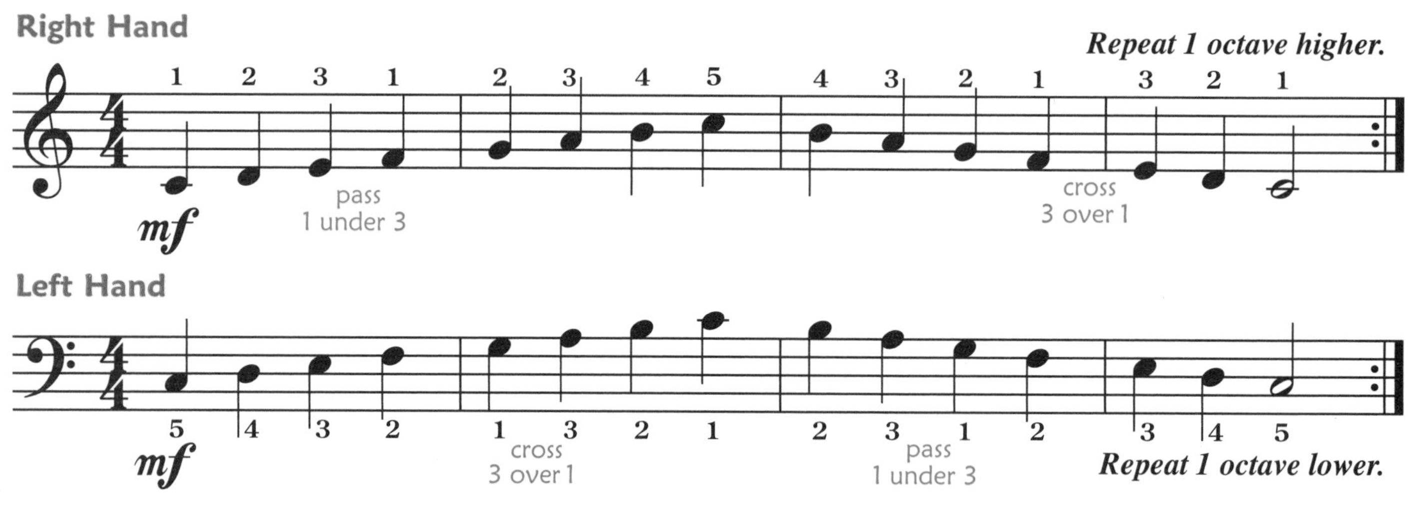

Workout 6 Intervals in the C Scale

Premier Performer *Play Workout 6 again one octave lower with the LH. Begin with finger 5.*

Theory Book: page 21

Workout 7 Preparation for the G Major Scale

Play 3 times each day.

G Major Scale

The G major scale contains 8 notes—
the G 5-finger pattern + 3 notes.

In the G major scale, there is one sharp—F♯.

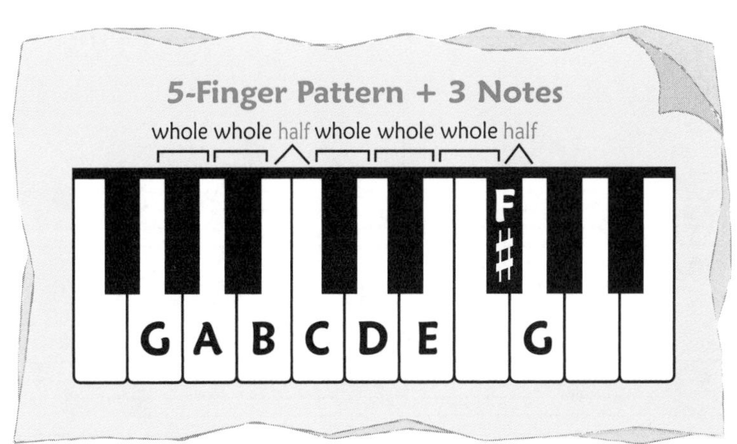

Playing the G Major Scale—Hands Separately

Say the finger numbers as you practice slowly. Memorize the fingering.

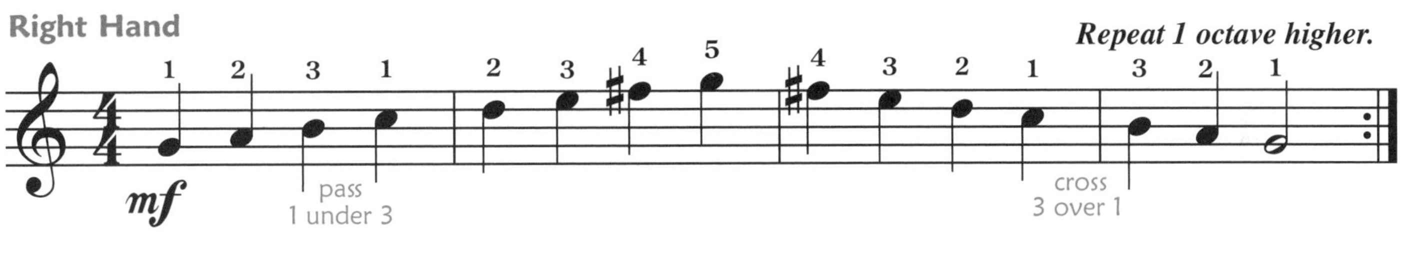

Workout 8 Intervals in the G Scale

Premier Performer *Play Workout 8 again* ***two*** *octaves lower with the LH. Begin with finger 5.*

Theory Book: page 22
Performance Book: pages 22–23

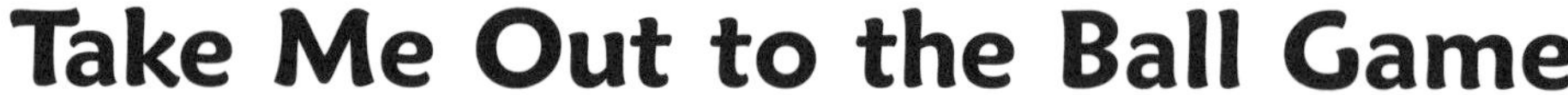

Take Me Out to the Ball Game

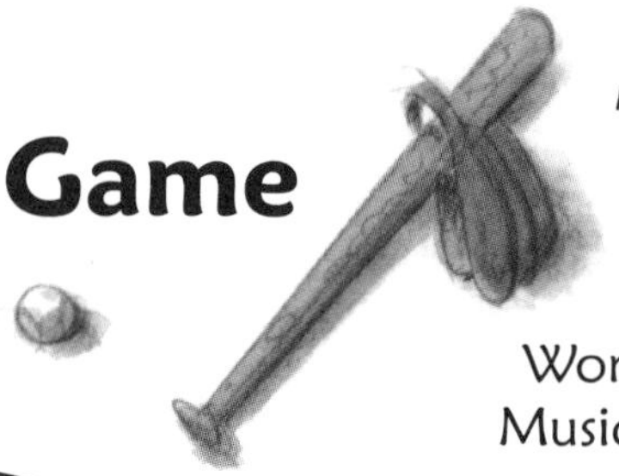

Words by Jack Norworth
Music by Albert von Tilzer

Lively
mf
7
Take me out to the ball game.
Take me out with the crowd.

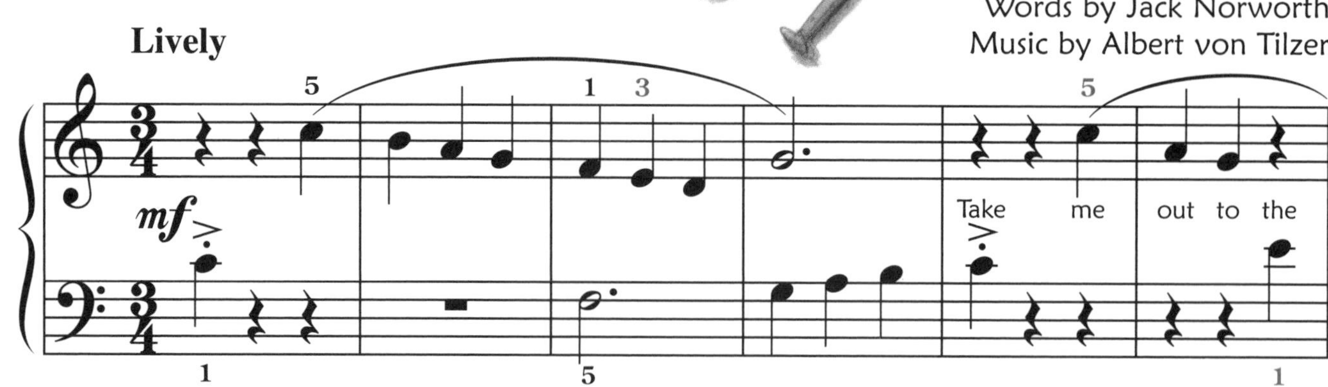

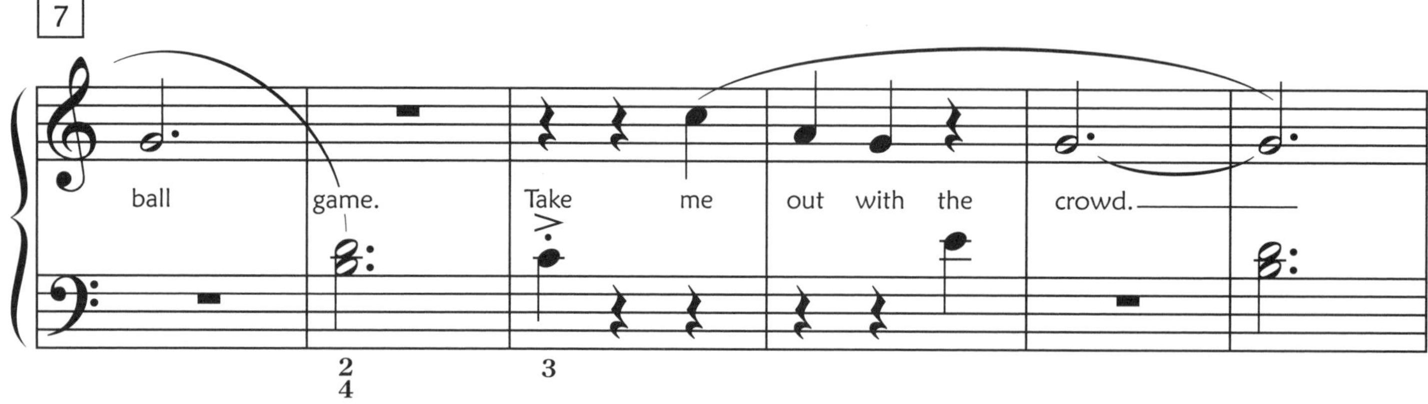

Duet: Student plays one octave higher.

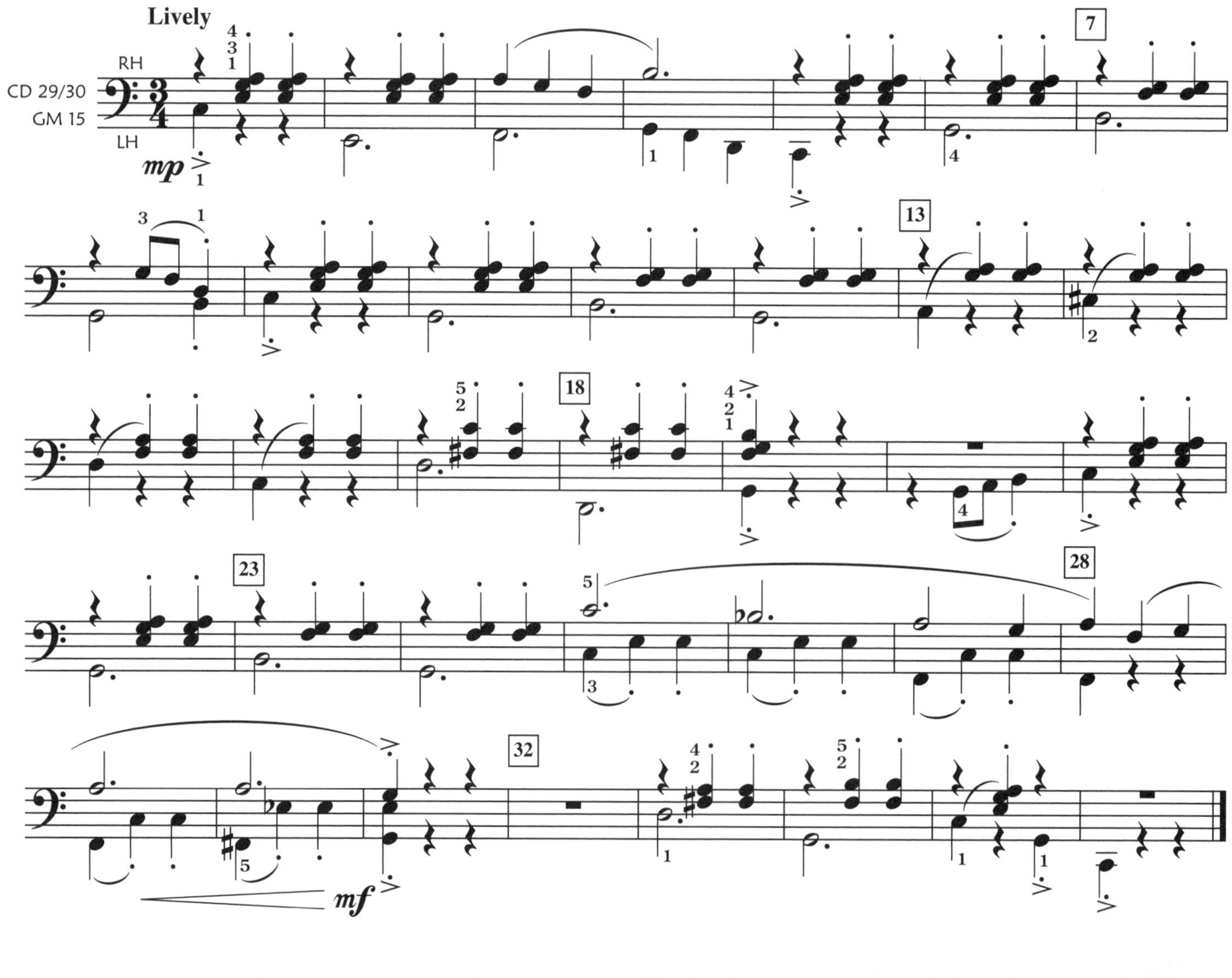

Lively
RH
CD 29/30
GM 15
LH
mp
7
13
18
23
28
32
mf

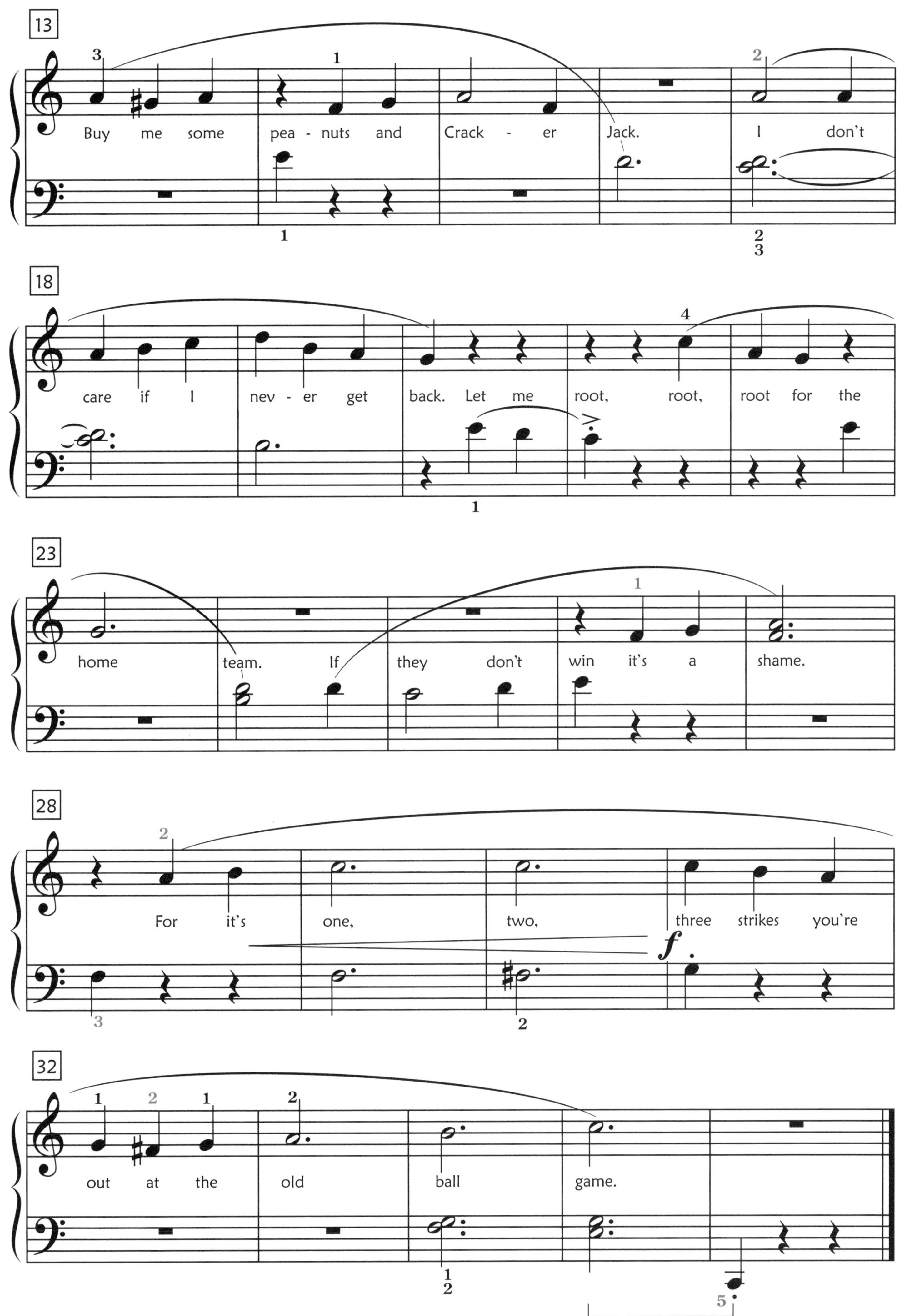
13
Buy me some pea - nuts and Crack - er Jack. I don't
18
care if I nev - er get back. Let me root, root, root for the
23
home team. If they don't win it's a shame.
28
For it's one, two, three strikes you're
32
out at the old ball game.

Theory Book: page 23

The Three-Note V^7 Chord in C

The 3-note **V** chord is built on the 5th note (dominant) of the scale. The $\mathbf{V^7}$ chord adds a 7th.

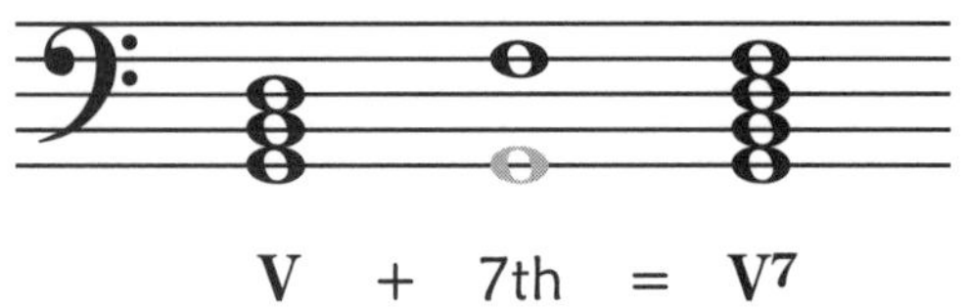

In C major, the $\mathbf{V^7}$ chord often omits the D (5th) and moves G up an octave.

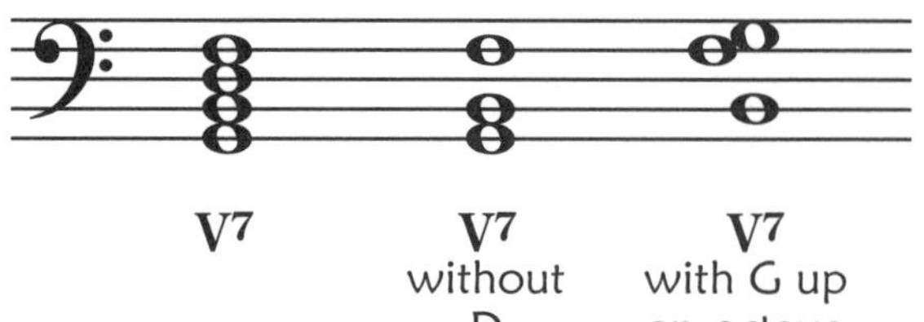

Moving from the I Chord to the Three-Note V7

Only 3 notes (G, B, F) of the chord will be used to play the $\mathbf{V^7}$ chord in this book.
To make the chord easier to play, the G is moved up an octave (B, F, G).
Use these three steps to play **I–V⁷**.

Step 1: Play the **I** chord.

Step 2: Raise the middle note a half step.

Step 3: Lower the bottom note a half step.

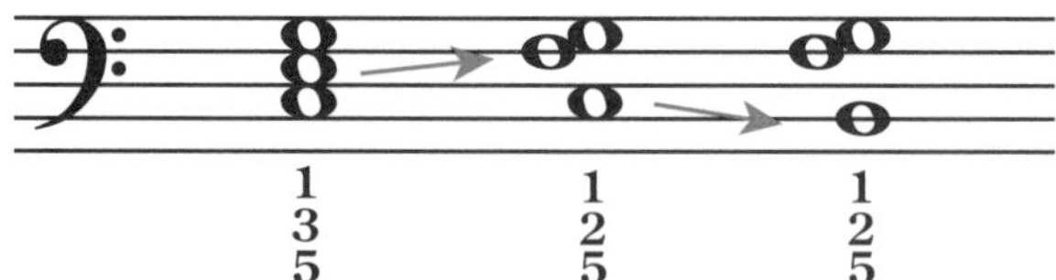

1. Play **I** and $\mathbf{V^7}$, saying the chord names aloud.

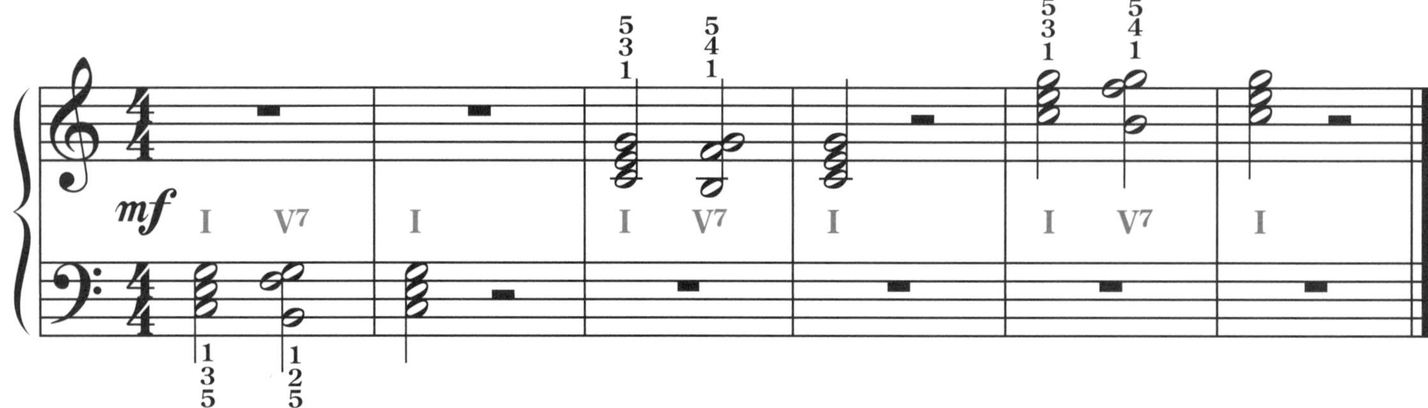

2. Using these rhythms, play **I** and $\mathbf{V^7}$ in C by reading the chord symbols.

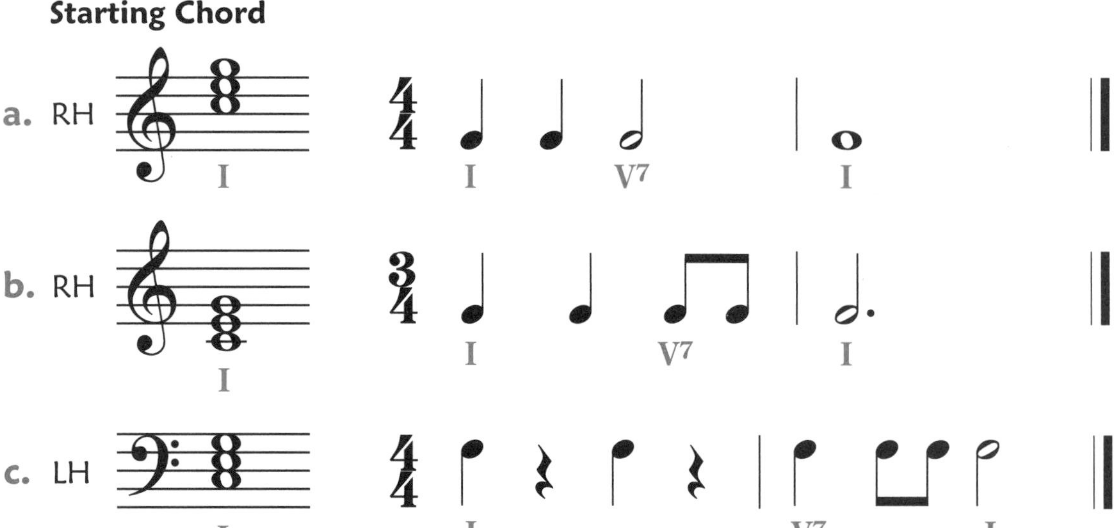

Theory Book: page 24

The Three-Note V7 Chord in G

The 3-note **V** chord is built on the 5th note (dominant) of the scale. The **V7** chord adds a 7th.

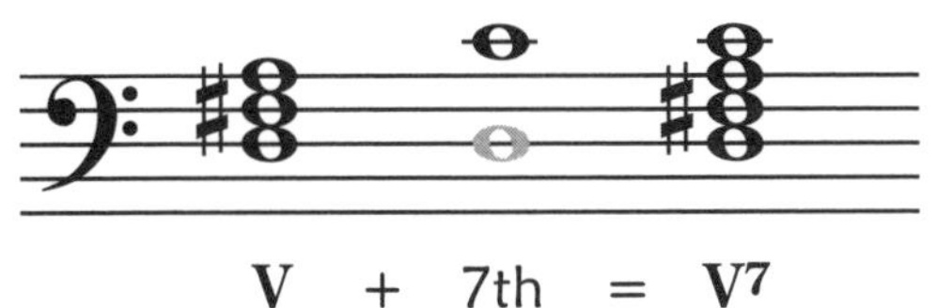

V + 7th = V7

In G major, the **V7** chord often omits the A (5th) and moves D up an octave.

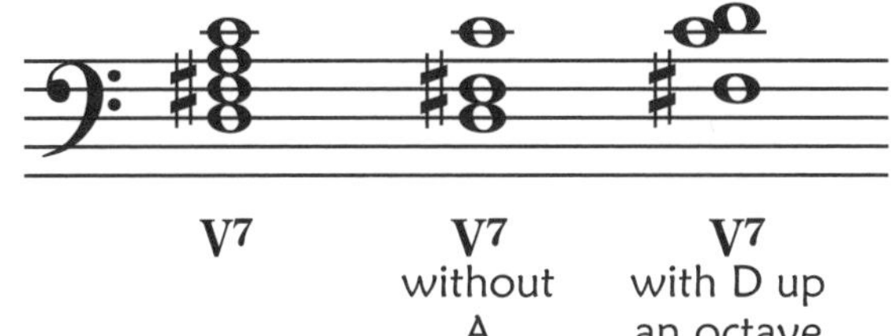

V7 | **V7** without A | **V7** with D up an octave

Moving from the I Chord to the Three-Note V7

Only 3 notes (D, F♯, C) of the chord will be used to play the **V7** chord in this book. To make the chord easier to play, the D is moved up an octave (F♯, C, D). Use these three steps to play **I—V7**.

Step 1: Play the **I** chord.

Step 2: Raise the middle note a half step.

Step 3: Lower the bottom note a half step.

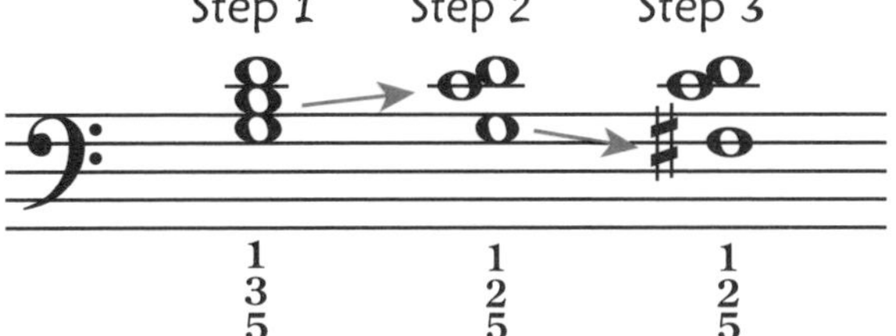

1. Play **I** and **V7**, saying the chord names aloud.

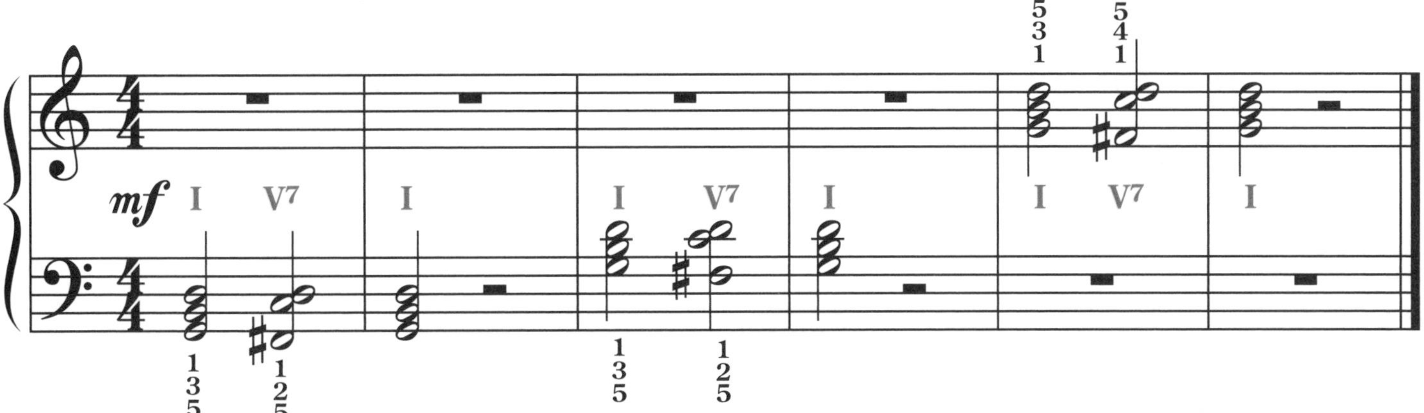

2. Using these rhythms, play **I** and **V7** in G by reading the chord symbols.

Starting Chord

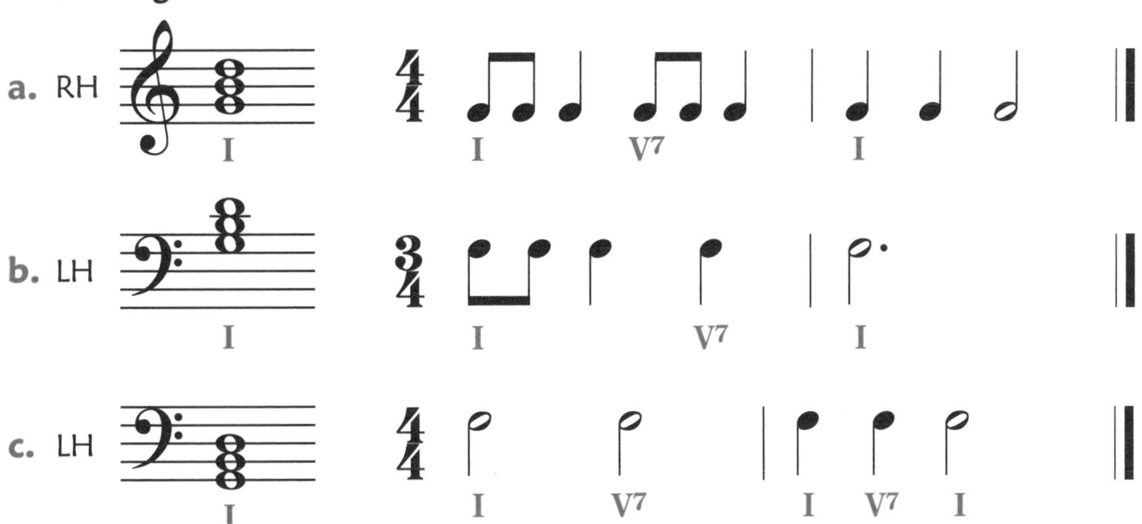

Theory Book: page 25
Performance Book: pages 24–25

Key Signature of G Major

F♯
F♯

1. In the G major scale, every F is played sharp.
2. Rather than place a sharp before every F, the sharp appears at the beginning of each staff. This is called the **key signature.**
3. All F's are played sharp unless cancelled by a *natural sign.*
4. A piece based on the G major scale is in the key of G major.

Scales My Way

CD 31/32 GM 16

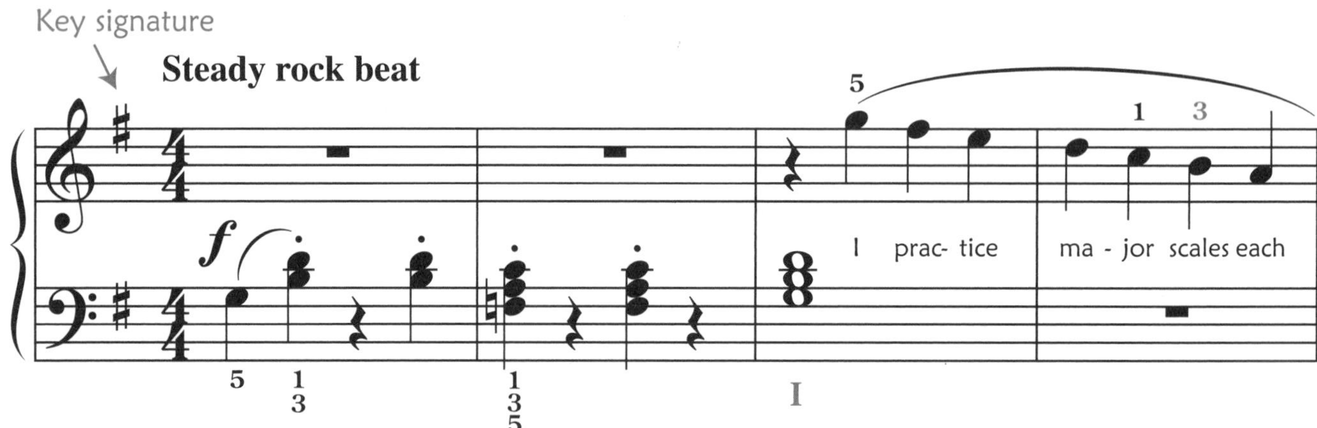
Key signature
Steady rock beat
I prac- tice ma - jor scales each
I

day.
And then I change them to "my

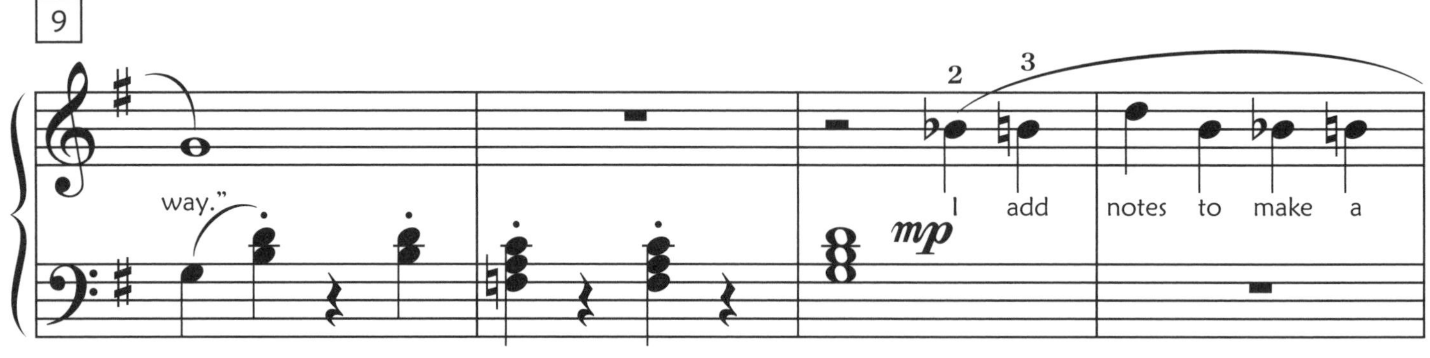
way."
I add notes to make a

Closer Look *Circle each F♯ in Scales My Way.*

Theory Book: page 26

Workout 9 RH Fingering Challenges

Play 3 times each day.

Over the Rainbow

(From the M-G-M Motion Picture "The Wizard of Oz")

Music by Harold Arlen
Lyric by E. Y. Harburg

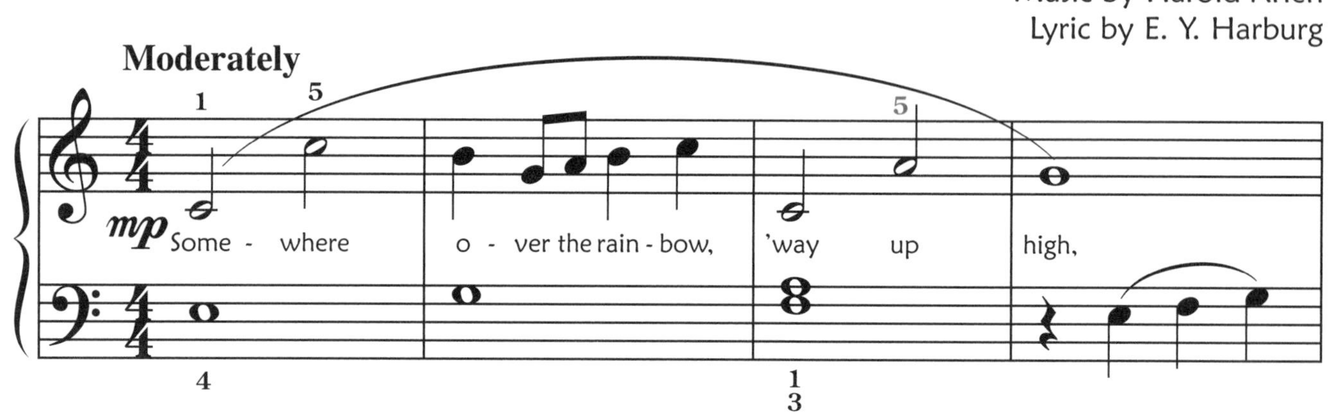

Duet: Student plays one octave higher.

5

stretch

there's a land that I heard of once in a lul - la - by.

9

f Some - where o - ver the rain - bow skies are blue,

13

and the dreams that you dare to dream real - ly do come true.

17

rit.

Use damper pedal when played without duet part.

Closer Look

Name the interval in the RH of measure 1. ______

Name the interval in the RH of measure 3. ______

Theory Book: pages 27–28
Performance Book: pages 26–27

Single Eighth Note and Eighth Rest

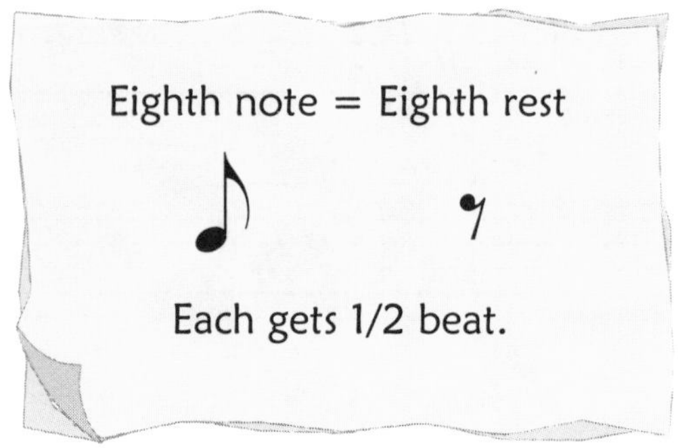

Clap and count each pattern 3 times each day.

Island Calypso

CD 35/36 GM 18

9

Out on the beach and wa-ter they spend the day hum-ming this is - land song:

13

stretch stretch

17

D.C. al Fine

Closer Look

Circle the [rhythm pattern] *rhythm pattern each time it appears in* Island Calypso.

Sight-Reading

Play and count aloud, once each day.

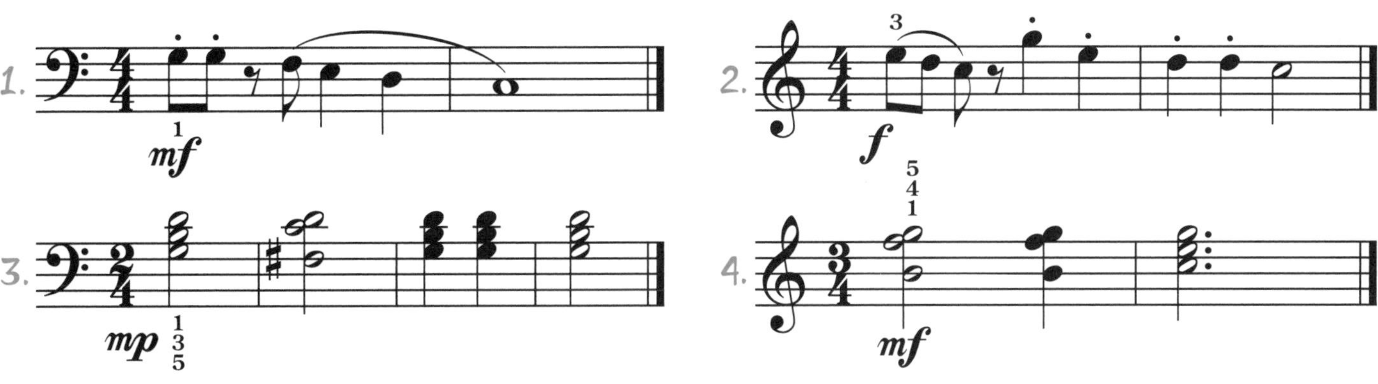

Theory Book: page 29

Dotted Quarter Note

A quarter note tied to an eighth note equals a dotted quarter note.

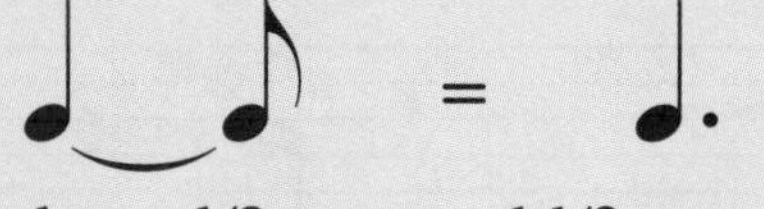

1 + 1/2 counts   1 1/2 counts

The dotted quarter note is almost always followed by an eighth note.

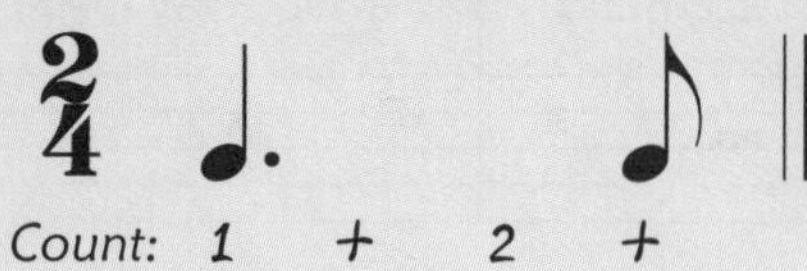

The dot increases the length of a note by half its value.

Clap and count each pattern 3 times each day.

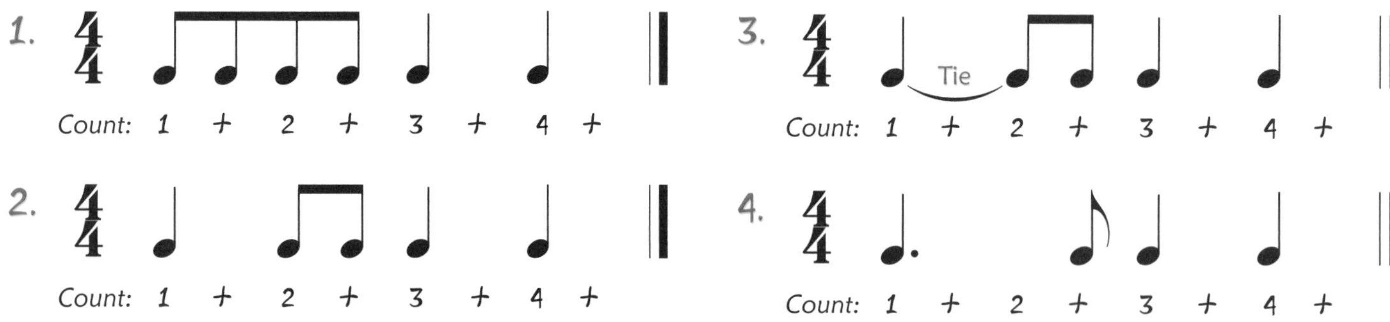

Note: Examples 3 and 4 above look different but sound alike.

Name That Tune!

Play these familiar Christmas melodies that use dotted quarter and eighth notes. Can you name them?

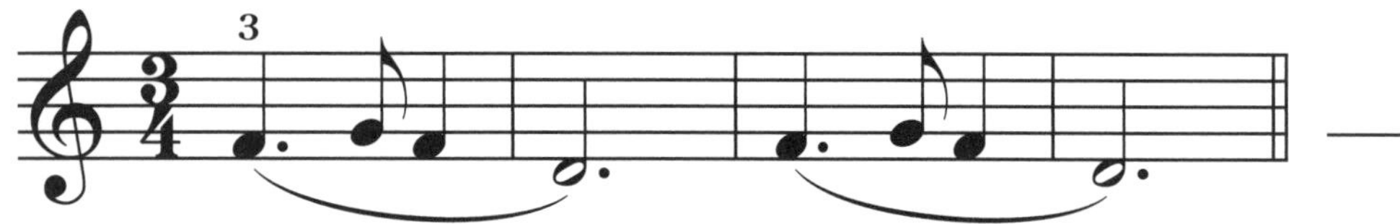

____

____

Premier Performer

Play the Name That Tune! *examples again one octave lower with the LH.*

Theory Book: page 30

Tap and count aloud 3 times each day.

Dutch Dance

Joachim van den Hove
(1567–1620)

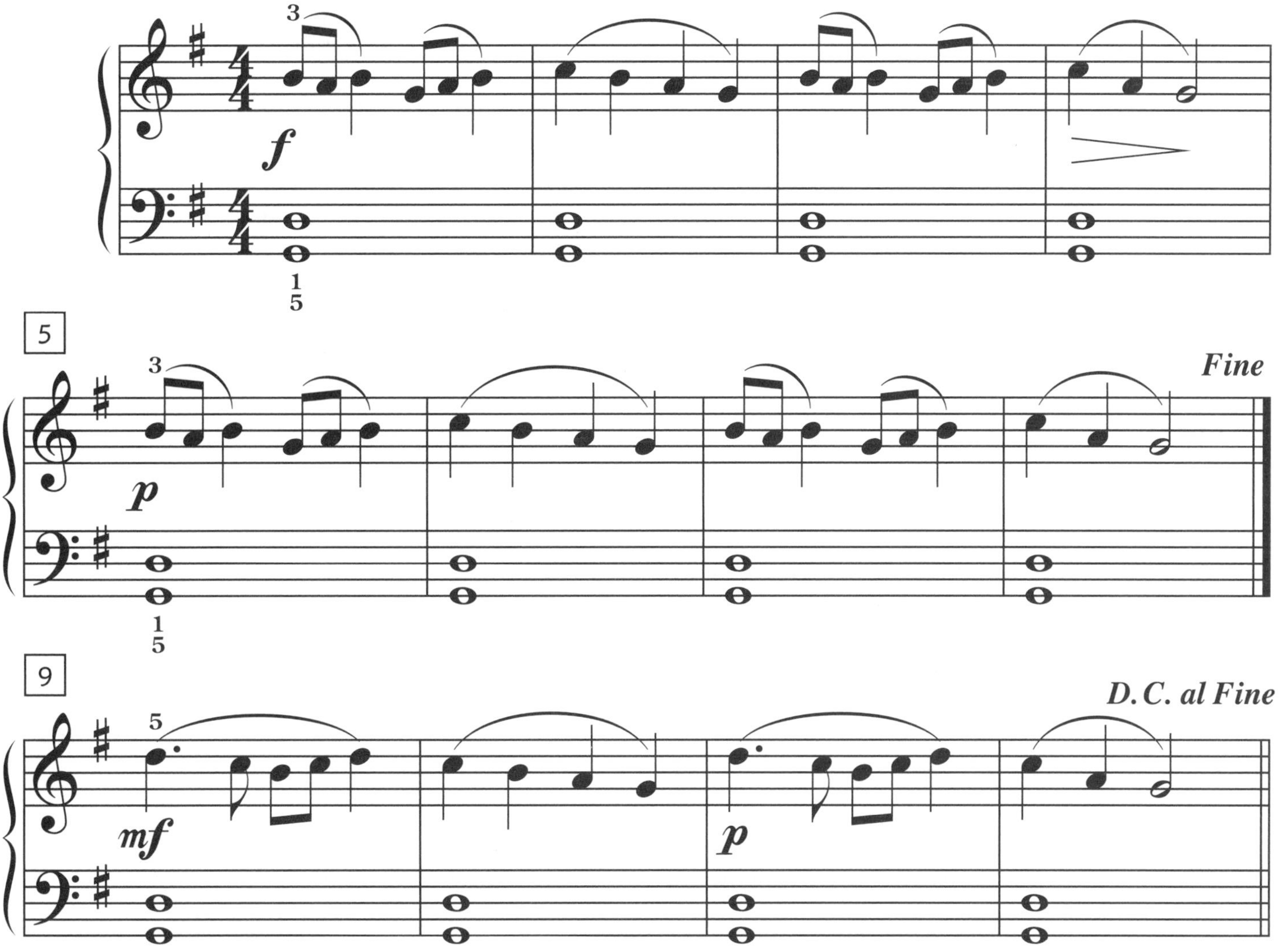

Moderato

3

f

1
5

5

3

p

1
5

Fine

9

5

mf

p

D.C. al Fine

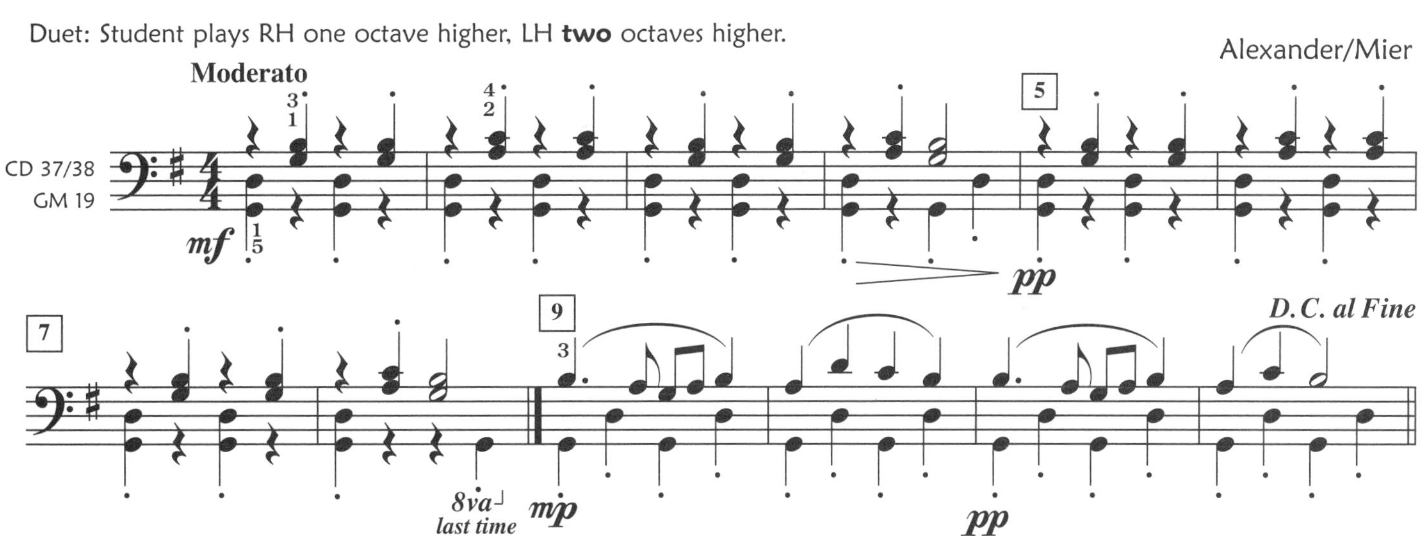

Theory Book: page 31
Performance Book: pages 28–29

Rhythm Workouts

On your lap, tap each rhythm 3 times daily as you count aloud.

1\. 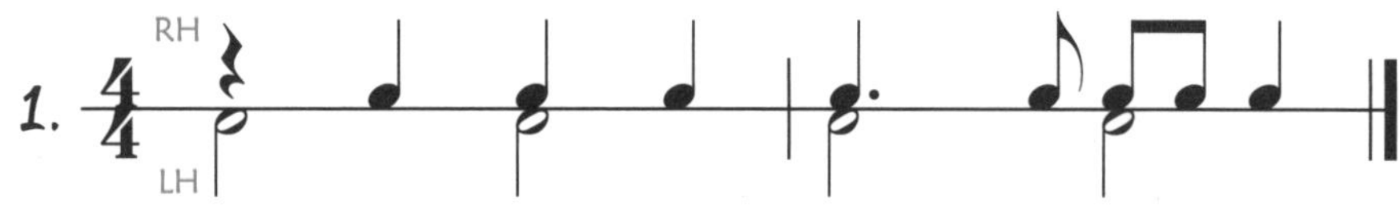

2\. 

Inspector Beauregard

CD 39/40 GM 20

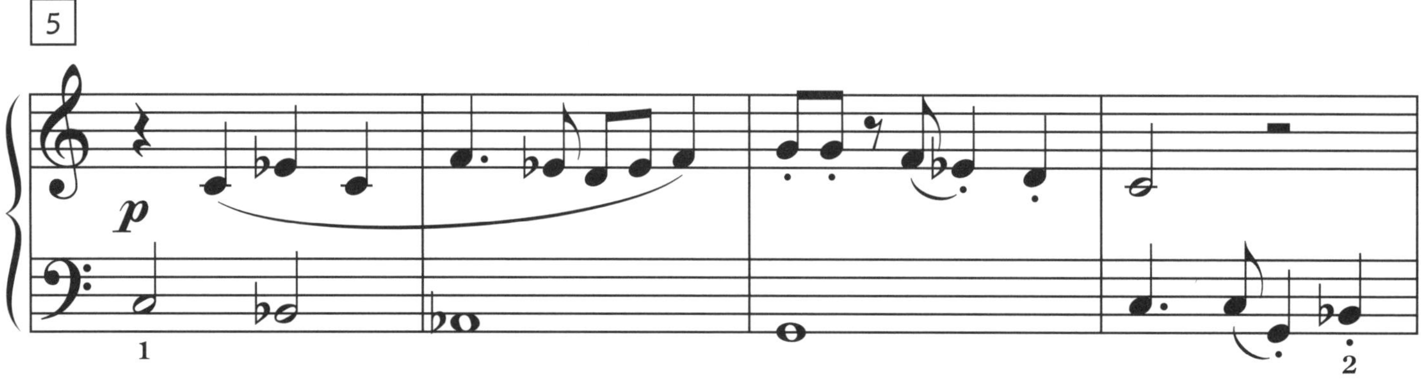

Sight-Reading

Play and count aloud, once each day.

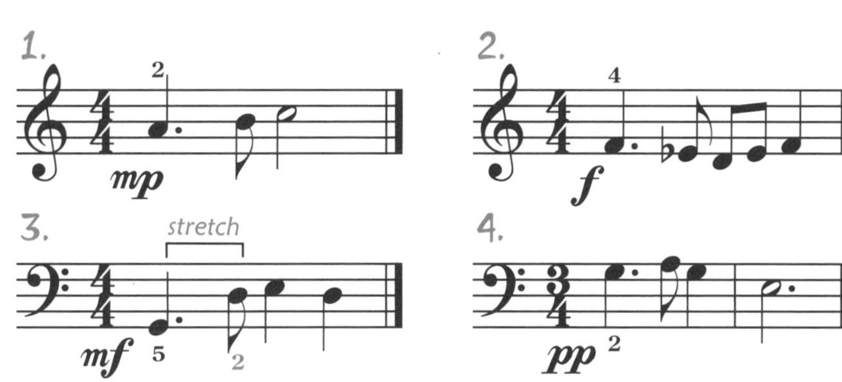

Theory Book: page 32
Performance Book: pages 30–31

Fiesta de España

CD 41/42 GM 21

Moderato

mp

mf

4

8

11

f

15

Fine

mf

19

ff

1 + 2 + 3 + 4 +

21

24

D.C. al Fine

mp

Premier Performer

Play the ♩. ♪♩ ♩ rhythm with careful counting.

Alfred's

Premier Performer

Piano Achievement Award

presented to

____

Student

You have
successfully completed
Lesson Book 2B
and are
hereby promoted to
Lesson Book 3.

____________________ ____________________

Teacher *Date*